D-Day
The Lost Evidence

D-Day
The Lost Evidence

Chris Going and Alun Jones

Crécy Publishing Limited

First published in 2004 by Crécy Publishing

A CIP record for this book is available from the British Library

Printed in England by Bath Press

ISBN 0 85979 097 5

Crécy Publishing Limited
1a Ringway Trading Estate, Shadowmoss Road, Manchester M22 5LH
www.crecy.co.uk

To those who fought, and those who fell, that we might live in freedom.

Contents

Prelude to invasion

By June 1944, the Second World War was already five years old in Europe. After the lightning *Blitzkrieg* advances across Europe and later into Russia in the early years of the war, Nazi Germany was now being gradually turned onto the defensive. In the east, the German forces in Russia had been fought to a standstill at a huge cost in lives and machinery. In the west, the exposed Atlantic coast of Europe, and in particular France, represented one of the most vulnerable faces of 'Fortress Europe'. Adolph Hitler had issued a directive to bolster the coastal fortifications of Europe as early as 1942. At the beginning of 1944, work on the so-called 'Atlantic Wall' took on new urgency after Hitler placed Field Marshall Erwin Rommel in command of defending the northern coast of France against the anticipated Allied invasion.

Rommel was the most popular German general of the Second World War. His inspections of the much-vaunted Atlantic Wall in December 1943 soon convinced him that it was far from the impregnable barrier that Nazi propaganda would have the world believe. He immediately ordered an urgent program of upgrading these fortifications – with bomb-proof concrete bunkers and gun emplacements, trenches, mines at sea and on land, fixed obstacles to rip apart boats on the beaches and gliders in the fields, and thousands of miles of barbed wire. It was Rommel's belief that to prevent a successful invasion of 'Fortress Europe', the invaders would have to be stopped on the beaches themselves, smashed against the Atlantic Wall, and thrown back into the sea before they could establish a beachhead.

In England, the operation to invade 'Fortress Europe' was led by General Dwight D Eisenhower. With experience of directing landings in North Africa and Italy, every ounce of his knowledge of large-scale operations would be needed if the Allies were to break the Atlantic Wall. Above all, the English Channel, which had prevented German forces over-running England in 1940, would now have to be crossed and the heavily defended beaches taken if the Allied forces were to liberate occupied Europe and advance into Germany. The shortest route across the English Channel led to Calais – so it is no surprise that this is where the Atlantic Wall was at its most complete and most deadly. Instead, the Allied planners opted for the beaches of Normandy, over 100 miles down the coast from Calais, in the hope of achieving a surprise landing.

The invasion plan – codename 'Operation Overlord' – combined the Allied air, sea and ground forces in what British Prime Minister Winston Churchill described as "the most difficult and complicated operation ever undertaken". The orders for Admiral Ramsay (naval Commander in Chief), for example, were over 1000 pages long. On the first day of the invasion over 130,000 men were to land in France in an operation involving over 7,000 ships and 11,000 aircraft. At one beach alone (Omaha) 8,000 vehicles were to come ashore in the first 24 hours.

If 'Overlord' was to have any chance of success, the Allied commanders had to have the best information available, both in planning the operation and in judging its progress once it was underway. And for that they were to rely, in a very large part, on the photographs bought back from above the battle.

The Images

For a few short hours on D-Day, June 6th 1944, aerial Photo Reconnaissance (PR) provided the best hope of judging the success or failure of the invasion, and on that day it seemed every pilot wanted to over-fly this small piece of airspace. These included Lt General Doolittle, Commander of the US 8th Air Force, in a P-38 Lightning and his second in command, Major General Earl Partridge. The 7th Photo Group's new Commanding Officer, Major Norris Hartwell, flew the first daylight sorties over the area with his second-in-command, returning the first reconnaissance images of the invasion. From RAF Northolt Air Commodore Geddes flew his Mustang and other RAF, Coastal Command and USAF reconnaissance Spitfires, Mustangs, Mosquitoes and Lightnings flew some 45 sorties over the beachheads that day and as many again managed objectives inland.

Once back in England at the bases of RAF Benson and RAF Northolt, and the US bases at Chalgrove and Mount Farm, the images were developed at the airfield and rushed to the plotting section of the Allied Central Interpretation Unit (ACIU) at RAF Medmenham, Buckinghamshire, where they were indexed, printed, and examined.

A Spitfire PR Mk XI of 16 Squadron RAF, 2nd Tactical Air Force (TAF) which flew sorties throughout the build-up to D-Day, and a further 16 sorties on June 6th alone. This particular aircraft (EN654) photographed rail centres in Amiens and Paris during D-Day.

An oblique Photographic Reconnaissance (PR) camera being loaded into an RAF Spitfire.

The D-Day imagery consisted of both vertical photographs (looking vertically down at the ground) and oblique photos (looking out of the side, or over the nose, of the aircraft). Some of the vertical photos were pieced together to create a mosaic of the beaches to give a single view of large stretches of the Normandy coast. Some of these pre D-Day mosaics have been reproduced in the book, however using modern computer techniques we have also created mosaics which have never been seen before.

Within days of the invasion, a handful of aerial reconnaissance images were released for use in newspapers and magazines. However, many of these images were of road and rail junctions and harbours miles away from the beaches. There are fewer good images than one might expect. The cameras on several aircraft were fitted with lenses of the wrong focal length, and bad weather and dull light meant that much of the earliest imagery is poor. And few aircraft flew the long straight photo 'legs' needed to create imagery suitable for making mosaics – at low level over the battlefield this would be an invitation to be shot down by anti-aircraft fire *(flak)*.

In the sixty years since they were taken, many of these original classified images have been mislaid, lost, or destroyed. First to go were many American print sets but some were taken back to the US. In England, the ACIU print library was transferred from RAF Medmenham in the 1960s.

The search for original imagery to accompany this book and television programme has turned up some of this lost treasure trove. In 1997 one of the writers found historic D-Day images in a non-descript box that gave no clue to the treasures within and in 2003, prints from another lost sortie came to light. This was flown by RAF Air Commodore Geddes and covered Sword, Juno and Gold beaches, continuing past the Omaha beachhead. But a full catalogue of sorties flown that day, compared with what now survives is less encouraging.

Much Coastal Command (106 Group) and 16 Squadron RAF imagery is gone forever, probably destroyed in the 1960's when many wartime British reconnaissance films were transferred from nitrate to safety film.

Surviving images from eight of the original D-Day sorties are reproduced in this book. They are 'uncontrolled' mosaics: multiple images fused and balanced to create panoramic views of the beaches without join lines, but they are not rendered map accurate. Never before published, and previously unseen by all but a privileged handful, these lost images are the true story of D-Day. As it happened.

P-38 'Lightning' aircraft of 370th Fighter Group, probably photographed at Andover airfield, Hampshire, showing their black and white 'invasion' stripes found on almost all Allied aircraft that flew in support of D-Day. A PR version of the P-38 – designated 'F-5' – was used for most USAF photographic reconnaissance during D-Day.

A Mosquito PR Mk XVI of 140 Squadron RAF, 2nd TAF. 140 Squadron, based at RAF Northolt, flew over 20 missions on D-Day.

The Fortifications

Aerial photographs were the primary means of obtaining detailed and accurate information on the fortifications along the Atlantic Wall. Over 1,000,000 individual photos, from some 3,000 separate flights or sorties, were taken of the French, Belgian and Dutch coastlines; in one day alone in Spring 1944 over 80 sorties contributed 24,000 photos. The staff of the Army Photographic Intelligence Section (APIS) often tasked sorties to seek out specific targets such as radar stations, railway marshalling yards, coastal fortifications and also specified the height at which the photographs should be taken. Some were taken at almost zero feet altitude, so close that personnel on the ground dived for cover as the aircraft passed. Others, particularly vertical photos, were taken at around 4–5,000ft. To disguise the invasion's true target beaches, twice as many PR flights were made over the area north east of the invasion area as over the intended landing beaches themselves.

Information from these photographs was later transferred onto tactical maps known as 'Bigots'. In addition, photographic enlargements of battery positions and strong points were produced and kept up-to-date. A separate detachment of the APIS was given the sole task of interpreting rail and road movements of enemy transport. Examination and interpretation of the photographs were often completed within hours of the aircraft landing and the results passed immediately to the Chiefs of Staff (CoS).

Aerial photos provided many significant intelligent breakthroughs in the build up to D-Day and the skills of the APIS staff were crucial to extracting this information.

A low-level vertical photo giving a highly detailed view of 4 medium casemates. Casemates were a new style of gun position used with light and medium guns along the Atlantic Wall. They consisted of a concrete bunker with a shelter at the rear to house personnel along with ammunition and a blunt-nosed casemate in the front for the gun. They were, to all intents and purposes, bomb-proof.

A vertical photo showing a coastal battery surrounded by houses, consisting of four medium casemates and six dummy gun sites. Traces of additional defensive systems such as trenches and barbed wire fences, can be seen in the sand.

A well-camouflaged battery of 170mm guns, only discovered by chance following a sortie which found a gun in a hedgerow. Further sorties were laid on and the development of this gun position was monitored over time.

The same battery, now showing considerable damage following naval and aerial bombardment. Two of the guns are destroyed; those remaining were disabled by their own crews shortly after June 6th.

A low-level picture of underwater obstacles, taken at low tide to enable accurate plotting of these structures. As late as February 1944, most of the Normandy coast was free of these barriers. Then, as ordered by Rommel, the Germans strove to strengthen them greatly: by June 1944 over 30 miles of underwater obstacles had been laid in the Overlord landing areas. The last intelligence report from aerial photography of these underwater obstacles was penned at 16.00 hours on June 5th 1944.

An oblique shot from the nose camera of a low-flying F-5 Lightning aircraft on a classic 'Dicing' sortie (from 'Dicing' with death) shows a group of men surprised at work erecting anti-landing stakes. Note the horse and cart in the middle with the men jumping off to take cover – also some men already lying down flat on the beach. In the background the 'hedgehog' anti-landing structures can be seen, many had mines attached to them.

Ground shot showing a German *Teller* anti-tank mine – one of 30,000 deployed – which has been mounted on top of a wooden stake. The steel spike attached to the stake behind is designed to rip the bottom of any boat or landing craft contacting it.

The low-lying fields behind the Normandy beaches were deliberately flooded to prevent troop and tank movement and confine attackers to isolated narrow roads along the tops of drainage channels or similar areas. These flooded areas took a heavy toll of US and British paratroopers on the night of June 5th-6th. These two images, taken on D-Day, show flooding inland from Le Grand Dune, and Le Mesnil, behind Utah Beach.

Radar was a significant problem to the Overlord planners. The array of radar stations along the French coast meant no seaborne approach to Normandy could remain secret; these electronic 'eyes' had to be neutralised if the landings were to succeed. For two and a half years prior to D-Day, Allied intelligence – under Dr R V Jones and Claude Wavell – continually mapped this network of radar stations. Eventually some 100 individual sites were attacked.

This picture from a forward facing camera in an RAF Spitfire shows a radar installation at Cherbourg La Brasserie consisting of a *Giant Wurzburg* (left) and a tall *Wasserman* (right). The *Wurzburg*, some 26 feet high and 23 feet wide, was designed to locate aircraft up to 50 miles away. The *Wasserman* was a mast-like structure 120 feet to 190 feet high but only 20 feet wide. Its role was to identify aircraft up to 180 miles away. Anti-glider stakes, so-called 'Rommel's asparagus', are in the foreground.

A detailed view of the radar complex at Douvres La Délivrande. The *Wasserman* radar at the bottom left of the photo is given away by its shadow. It is surrounded by a two-layer defensive trench system with three gun batteries. *Freyas* and *Wurzburgs* occupy the ground to the middle and right of the photo. A formidable defensive system encloses the whole radar complex with light anti-aircraft guns, defensive trenches, bunkers and strong points.

A very low-level RAF photograph of the radar station at Le Havre (Cap de La Héve). This shows a *Freya* (left) and a *Giant Wurzburg* (right), note the person running to safety between the building and the *Freya*. The *Freya* radar was excellent at picking up surface craft up to 125 miles away.

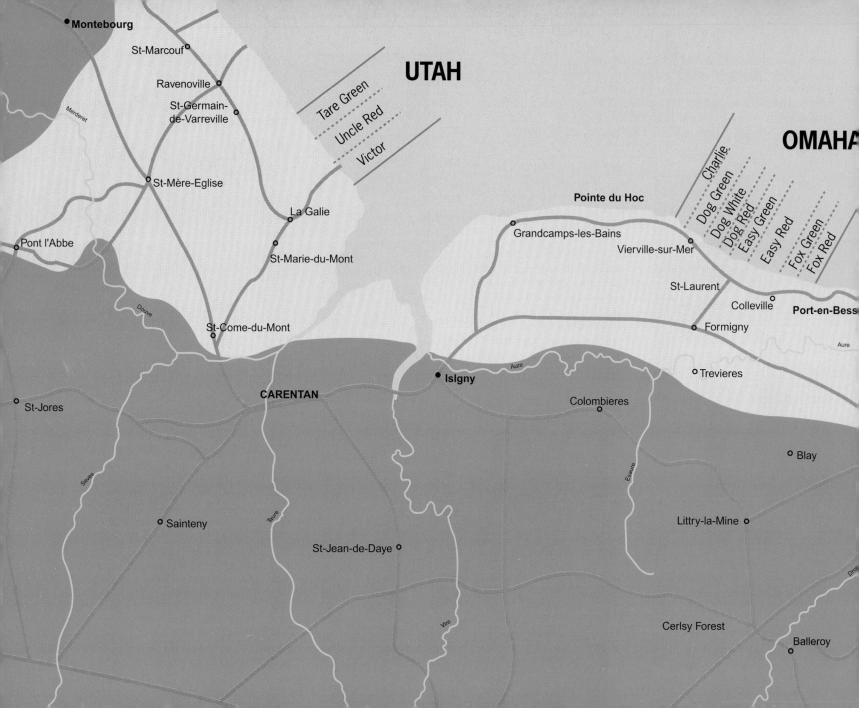

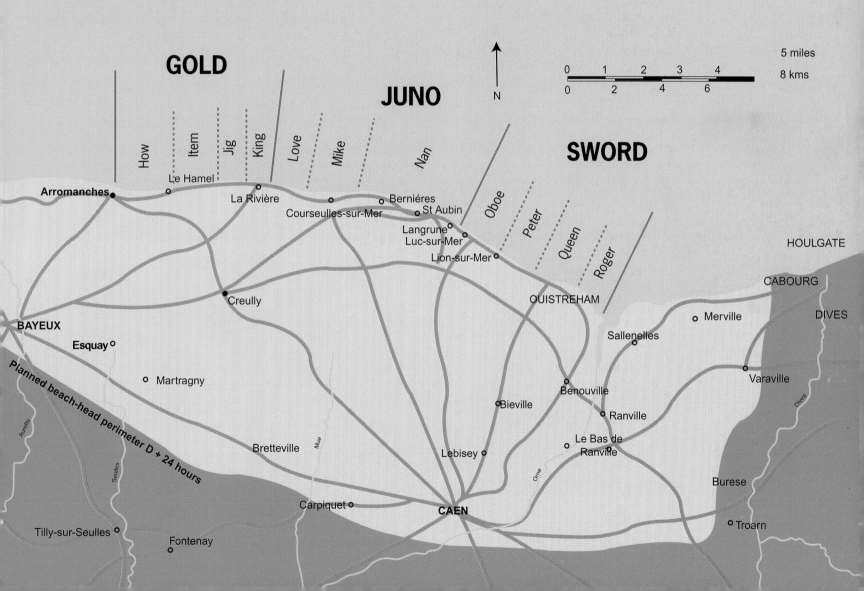

The Beaches

GOLD

JUNO

N

SWORD

5 miles
8 kms

0 1 2 3 4

0 2 4 6

How

Item

Jig

King

Love

Mike

Nan

Oboe

Peter

Queen

Roger

Arromanches

Le Hamel

La Rivière

Courseulles-sur-Mer

Berniéres

St Aubin

Langrune

Luc-sur-Mer

Lion-sur-Mer

HOULGATE

CABOURG

Creully

OUISTREHAM

DIVES

BAYEUX

Merville

Sallenelles

Esquay

Varaville

Martragny

Benouville

Bieville

Ranville

Aurette

Planned beach-head perimeter D + 24 hours

Le Bas de Ranville

Seulles

Bretteville

Mue

Lebisey

Burese

Orne

Dives

Carpiquet

CAEN

Troarn

Tilly-sur-Seulles

Fontenay

Landing Craft Assaults (LCAs) in mass formation.

Utah

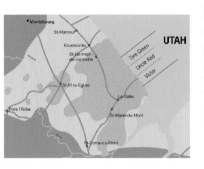

The most westerly of the invasion beaches, Utah was to bring US forces ashore right on the Cotentin peninsular to protect the flank of the invasion force. The amphibious landings were to be supported with parachute drops behind the beaches by US 82nd and 101st Airborne Division paratroopers.

A mosaic showing approximately two miles of the planned landing site for Utah. The photographs, taken on April 23rd 1944, show the low-lying terrain – there are no cliffs to impede invaders – however the very dark patches in the fields behind the beach show that the Germans have flooded this area. There are fortified positions at both ends of the beach and in the middle. Fresh earthworks to the middle left show trench systems under construction and the triangular mark to the middle right of the photo reveals a longer established defensive site at La Madeleine.

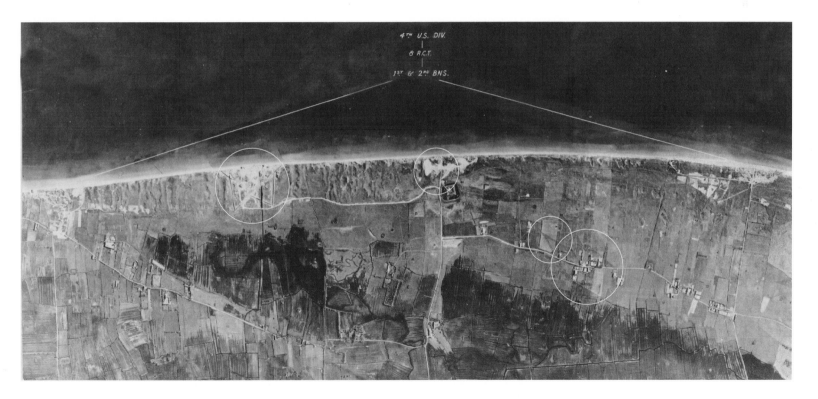

Pointe du Hoc

One of the most dangerous German gun positions was a battery of six 155mm guns at Pointe du Hoc. With an estimated range of 20,000 yards these guns could shell Omaha, just to the east; Utah, six miles to the northwest; and the US naval units stationed off them. On April 15th 1944 Pointe du Hoc was attacked by the US 9th Air Force. The site was again plastered on June 4th and attacked once more during the night of June 5th-6th by RAF Bomber Command. The bombing also churned up the beach and blew scree from the cliffs.

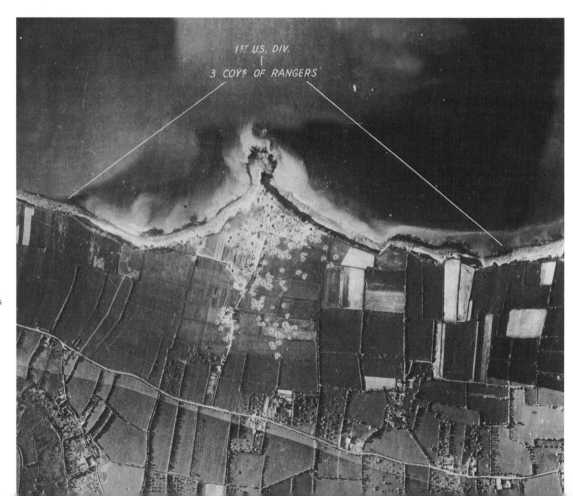

A mosaic of the Pointe du Hoc area taken from photography flown on May 23rd 1944 showing the results of the USAF attack on April 15th. This image shows how much of the landscape has been obliterated by the bombing. The steep cliffs and rocky shoreline are evident and the length of shadow gives some indication as to the height of the cliffs. Ten days after this imagery was taken, the guns were pulled back to avoid further damage from aerial bombardments.

OMAHA

Omaha

Omaha was the more easterly of the two American beaches. The designated area was the only sandy stretch of coast in a distance of over 25 miles. Here United States forces faced a 7,000 yard wide concave beach, its western third fronted by a sea wall some 4-6 feet high, and the eastern two-thirds covered by a slippery shingle bank. Just inland the ground rises to a 100-foot high plateau. The coast here is easily defensible – to reach this higher ground attackers from the sea would have to pass up four shallow valleys known as 'draws'. At its eastern and western ends the beach is flanked by promontories giving defenders a clear view along it. During the morning of D-Day a force of 34,000 men would be landed in several waves, reinforced in the afternoon by a further 24,000 men. The plan was for the troops to be off the beach and at the top of the plateau within an hour of coming ashore, and six miles inland by the end of the day. To do this US troops would first have to force their way up these valleys (Draws) past flanking German strong points (*Wiederstandnesten*). As if that was not enough, during the day military engineers would have to prepare the rough tracks running up the exits for the 8,000 military vehicles of all types due to use them in the next 24 hours.

This RAF mosaic taken on April 27th 1944 shows the Vierville sur Mer section at the western end of Omaha beachhead. This was assigned to the US 29th Division and the US 1st Division (Rangers). The dark shadow along the cliff line that falls onto the beach gives some indication as to the height of the cliffs in this area. To the far left there is evidence of German defensive positions in place and to the far right evidence of new positions being constructed. Note the white roads and white surface of recently disturbed earthworks near the valley on the far right. This valley is the Vierville draw (draw D1) along which the main breakout from this section of Omaha beach was to be achieved.

AREA
ST. LAURENT S/M
TAKEN BY 140 Sqd
DATE 27.4.44.

MAP SHEET 0S.GS.4347
MAP SQUARE Sht.34/8.N.E.
MAP SQUARE CO-ORDS {673918. 695906
661/895. 682883}

MOSAIC No (x) 2072   NEG No 59886.

1ST U.S. DIV.

16 RCT.

APPROXIMATE SCALE LINE

200 100 0   200   400   600   800
YDS.
MILES.   ½ MILE

Mosaic of 1st (U.S.) Div.
(16 R.C.T.)

This section of Omaha beachhead was code-named
'Dog' beach and was designated to the US 1st Division. A
large anti-tank trench has been built across the mouth of
the draw and numerous other defensive works are in
progress along the beach, characterised by the bright
white patches of earthwork and roads.

An oblique photograph of the strong point in the centre of Port en Bessin
halfway between Omaha and Gold beaches. A wall can be seen at the lower
right hand side of the photo blocking the main road off the beach and a
defensive tower is situated across on it's left hand side. All exits off the beach are
also blocked and workers are walking in gangs close to the sea front.

Another part of Port en Bessin with the
beach exits clearly blocked by a
concrete wall.

Towards the rear of Port en
Bessin a large anti-tank ditch
cuts across a railway line that
disappears into a hillside to the
right of the photo. This highly
defended town was not attacked
as part of the initial landings on
D-Day.

Gold

Some 15 miles east of Omaha beachhead, the Gold sector ran from Port en Bessin in the west to La Rivière in the east, divided into sectors Item, Jig and King. Here, unlike at Omaha, the terrain inland was flat marshland with transverse roads. It too was well defended, with strong points at Le Hamel, *Wiederstandnesten* (WN 37), at Cabane Des Douanes in front of Les Roquelles (WN 36), at the west end of King Green (WN 35), slightly inland between La Rivière and Mont Fleury (WN 34), and at La Rivière (WN 33).

A photo mosaic of Gold Beach, where the 50th Northumbrian Division of the British Army would be landed on D-Day. The imagery, compiled from a 140 Squadron RAF sortie flown on March 20th 1944, shows the beach area between the towns of Le Hamel to the left and La Rivière to the right. This is again a low-lying coastal flat; the dark patches in the centre indicate flooded fields. Although there are few signs of any defensive systems when this photo was taken, by D-Day the Atlantic Wall here had been considerably strengthened.

A major strong point was in the town of Le Hamel, at the west end of Gold beach. A large anti-tank ditch is being constructed at the edge of the town and the main strong point is on the sea wall in a large square building. The locations of these features and their characteristics, as far as Allied intelligence could establish them, were all transferred to intelligence maps for use in the preparation on the landings on Gold beach and elsewhere.

Juno

A mosaic of the eastern edge of Juno beach around the town of Berniéres showing the planned landing area of the 8th Canadian Brigade. There is a low-lying beach area, very narrow at high tide, and a number of major defensive positions situated in the town including minefields, pill boxes, anti-tank ditches and other strong points.

A mosaic of the Juno beach area at Courseulles assigned to the 7th Canadian Brigade on D-Day. The main town is adjacent to the dock and diverted river, with low-lying fields and farmland surrounding the town. There is little beach area at the mouth of the river. Most of the landing would have to take place on the wider parts of the beach further away to the left and right.

Sword

A mosaic of Sword beach created from aerial photography flown before D-Day. The image date is the date the mosaic was originally made, not when the photography was taken. The image shows an area from the town of Lion-sur-Mer on the left to La Bréche on the right, and a beach that is very flat with major defensive systems under construction at the centre just behind the beach. The dark patches in the fields behind the beaches indicate more flooding. This part of the beach would be designated on D-Day to the 2nd East Yorkshire and 1st South Lancashire Regiments of the British 3rd Infantry Division.

The gun positions at Franceville Plage, opposite the Orne estuary on the eastern end of Sword overlooking the beach. The dark black line represents an anti-tank ditch. The strong point – which is incomplete – is in the upper middle left of the photo.

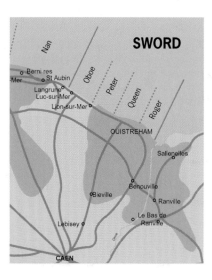

For several weeks before the invasion, Allied aircraft began 'softening up' operations against guns, radar and transportation targets in the planned landing areas. To keep their intentions veiled, many sites outside Normandy also had to be attacked; something like ten times more raids were carried out closer to Calais – the area the Allies wanted the Germans to believe would be the real target of the landings – than in Normandy. It was only just before the invasion itself that a furious bombardment of the Normandy fortifications was unleashed. During the night of June 5-6th, RAF Bomber Command despatched 1012 aircraft to bomb coastal batteries behind the five invasion beaches, and at first light the 1st, 2nd and 3rd Air Divisions of the US 8th Air Force continued the assault on the beach defences. During the morning assault, 3096 tonnes of bombs were dropped. Later in the day the USAF alone dropped a further 1647 tonnes of bombs.

Gun Emplacements

Medium casemates at Mont Fleury, just behind Sword beach. Here two have been built and roofed and two are under construction. At the top of the photo is a large anti-tank trench. Minefields are visible because of stunted grass growth above the shallowly buried mines, leaving regular rows of small white dots which were mapped by Allied intelligence.

Nearly all gun batteries along the Normandy coast were identified through aerial photography alone. This vertical photo shows a group of six heavy guns at Crisbecq, northwest of Utah beach. There are also six dummy guns with various types of wire barrier surrounding the battery itself.

The same battery, photographed on D-Day after the final air bombardment.

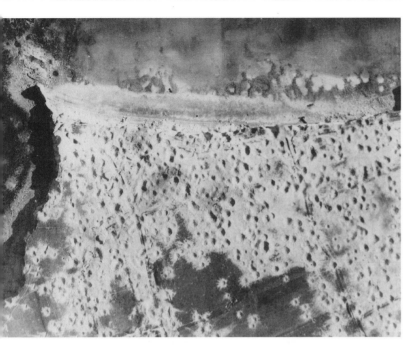

The four gun casemates at Pointe du Hoc following a heavy air bombardment on the night of 5th-6th June. Had the guns not been damaged by aerial bombing and moved back from their positions on June 3rd they could have caused havoc to the troops landed on Omaha beach during D-Day. This image shows the heavily cratered landscape; 'like the moon' in the words of one veteran which created problems for the assault teams. All landmarks had effectively been destroyed, so navigating and moving around the heavily cratered area was very difficult.

Training

As the softening-up continued, the Allied troops trained for D-Day. In the images below, troops are crammed into a Landing Craft Infantry – LCI. During one such training exercise on the night of 27th-28th April at Slapton Sands, Devon, German E-boats got amongst the landing ships and attacked them – leaving over 1000 men killed or wounded. The significance of the exercise taking place at Slapton Sands was not lost on Hitler. He recognised the similarities between this beach and those along the Normandy coastline between Le Havre and Cherbourg – the very area earmarked for the invasion. Nevertheless, both he and Rommel continued to believe that the invasion was most likely to come ashore around Calais.

Training on the south coast was as realistic as possible using live rounds and high explosives. This picture shows an unusually large and perhaps unintended explosion.

Railways

Isolating Normandy from the French railway network was vital. Reconnaissance photos were used to identify targets, assess troop movements, and measure damage and repair rates. This is a marshalling yard in Orleans, France, in the immediate aftermath of an air raid. Bomb craters cover the whole photo and destroyed trains and rolling stock cover the central section of the yard. Smoke rises from burning wagons.

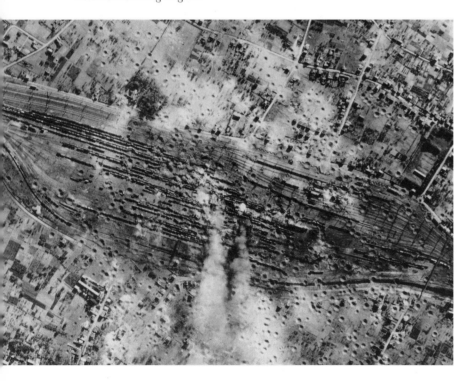

Strategic points along the railway lines were also attacked. South of Normandy at Saumur, between Angers and Niort, a railway tunnel has been attacked with massive 12,000lb 'Tallboy' bombs to thwart deployment of the 17 SS *Panzergrenadiers*. Dropped by 617 Squadron RAF (the Dambusters) the bombs have left massive impact craters on either side of the tunnel entrance and two have destroyed the railway line just outside it. A direct hit on the tunnel itself has blown the roof in and put the line permanently out of action.

Radar

Attacks began against radar stations on May 10th 1944 and by June 5th only a handful of 47 coastal stations were still operating. The staff of these still-working stations, demoralised and confused by the determined attacks, were almost all deceived by the Electronic Counter Measures (ECM) flown during the night of June 5th-6th by RAF 617 Squadron. Attacks against the radar stations were pressed home with great daring and courage. During one attack near Le Havre, an RAF pilot, hit by *flak*, deliberately dived his aircraft into the radar mast to destroy it. Air Staff agreed that the pilot should be awarded a posthumous Victoria Cross, but his identity was never confirmed.

The effect of air attacks on a *Freya* radar station on the coast at Pointe et Raz de La Percee, three miles east of Pointe du Hoc. At the centre of the photograph is a circular protective wall containing a now collapsed *Freya* radar station.

An RAF strike on radar stations at St Vaast La Pernelle. The main sites on the left and top of the photo are under attack and plumes of smoke can be seen rising following the bomb impacts. One radar mast, nicknamed Windjammer, remains intact on the right hand side. It was destroyed by later air attacks.

The outline invasion plan was completed in April 1944, and as more detailed planning continued, the invasion armada began forming up in southern England under conditions of the highest secrecy. Eisenhower set the invasion date as the June 5th, and loading began in earnest at the end of May. However, in the early hours of Sunday June 4th, after the naval forces had begun to set sail, Eisenhower received a weather briefing from meteorologist Group Captain Stagg. It was not good news. June 5th promised to be stormy, with low cloud, rough seas and force five winds. Eisenhower decided to postpone Operation Overlord for one day, to see how the weather developed. When the 'return to base' order reached some of the leading minesweepers, they were almost within sight of the French coast.

In the early hours of Monday June 5th Eisenhower received a more optimistic weather briefing from Stagg, although it was still far from certain. After agonising over the options, he said simply: "OK, let's go."

View from a radarscope on board an US 8th Air Force bomber approaching the Normandy coast on the morning of June 6th 1944: D-Day. The aircraft is at the centre of the picture, marked by the large white area in the centre, Le Havre is to the right and the invasion coast shows as a white line. The mass of white 'echoes' above the coastline reveal the invasion fleet.

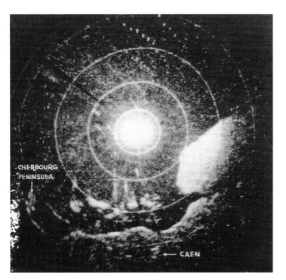

US Army troops march aboard a Landing Craft Infantry (Large) (LCI (L)) at an invasion port in England, June 1944.

Our landings in the Cherbourg to Le Havre area have failed. I have withdrawn the troops.

My decision to attack at this time and place was based on the best information available. The troops, the airmen and the Navy did all that bravery and devotion to duty could do.

If any blame or fault attaches to the attempt, it is mine alone.

Eisenhower's own hand-written press release prepared on June 5th, after giving the order for Operation Overlord to commence. It was to be issued if the invasion failed.

Pegasus Bridge

The German tank units stationed east and south of Caen were an ever-present threat to the left flank of the invasion forces. To prevent them moving in over the River Orne and attacking the invasion force, British airborne forces were tasked with seizing the two bridges over the Orne

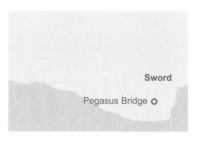

Sword

Pegasus Bridge ○

and its canal before the invasion landed, and holding them until reinforcements could arrive. Six 'Horsa' gliders of the Oxfordshire and Buckinghamshire Light Infantry, led by Major John Howard, spearheaded the attack on Pegasus bridge just a few minutes after midnight on the morning of June 6th. Three landed within yards of the entrance to the bridge over the canal. A fourth landed 400 yards to the east, however two others landed 5 and 10 miles away leaving their troops with a long night-time trek. In the first clash of D-Day Howard's force captured Pegasus bridge and held it awaiting reinforcements. The majority of the later glider reinforcements have landed in Landing Zone 'N', which includes the field near the road on the right of the photo.

I think practically all of us, without exception, thought that we were on a suicide mission. Personally I was frightened to death. I was sitting in my seat in the glider and my teeth were chattering, my knees were knocking – I was really scared to death, because I felt a bit like the convicted man when he's been waiting to be taken out to the scaffold. I thought, "Well, you know, this is my last time on Earth, and I'll probably die within the next hour or two." So I was really frightened.

Denis Edwards, British Oxfordshire and Buckinghamshire Light Infantry

An RAF Halifax V towing a Horsa glider. The airfield to the left of the Halifax is RAF Tarrant Rushton, from where many of the Horsas were towed.

1 Gliders Chalk 1, 2 & 3 within yards of Pegasus bridge
2 Horsa glider Chalk 5
3 Landing Zone N

The 140 Squadron RAF reconnaissance photo opposite was taken shortly after the landings of the British 6th Airborne Division near the bridges over the River Orne (left) and Caen canal (middle). The coast at Ouistreham lies three miles to the north, to the top in this picture.

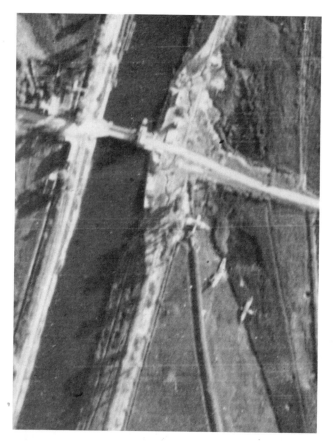

In a fine piece of flying, three of the six Horsa gliders touch down just after midnight at Pegasus bridge. This reconnaissance photo shows gliders Chalk 1, 2 and 3 where they came to rest, within yards of the bridge.

Horsa glider Chalk 5, seen here, lands close enough for its occupants to play a significant part in seizing these two first, vital D-Day objectives. Both bridges fell by about 00.35 hours and soon after the incongruous code words, 'Ham and Jam', crackled across the ether signifying success.

Pegasus bridge, with two of the three leading Horsa gliders visible in the background.

Later on D-Day, glider reinforcements under Major General Richard Gale are landed to back up the Major Howard's force. This is the edge of one of their designated landing areas, Landing Zone 'N'.

British troops leaving a Horsa glider in their Jeep.

A British Bren Carrier being offloaded from a Hamilcar glider (here, at RAF Tarrant Rushton). Hamilcars could carry two of these Carriers and were used to fly in vehicles as part of Gale's reinforcements.

Merville Battery

1 Fierce bombing close to the Merville battery
2 Merville battery after the RAF bombardment

British intelligence had identified two batteries with coastal guns. One at Franceville Plage was unfinished, but the complex near Merville village was thought to have guns that threatened the invasion at Sword and, at extreme range, even Juno beachhead.

Merville was to be taken in the early hours of D-Day by 9th Battalion, British 6th Airborne Division, led by Lt Colonel Otway. The bulk of the 750-strong force were to land by glider and parachute a mile or so from the battery and then advance to surround the battery after it had been bombed by the RAF. The assault would begin when a further three gliders, carrying 70 specially selected volunteers – all unmarried men – landed against the walls of the Merville battery, between the guns themselves.

If the taking of Pegasus bridge was an example of a battle plan working out in almost every detail, the attack on Merville battery could not have been more different.

Sword
Merville Battery O

Aerial photography, in my view, played such a critical role that I don't think I would have been successful without it. We owe a hell of a lot to the Royal Air Force, not only for the risks they took getting those photographs, but the courage that they showed taking us in.

Lt Colonel Terence Otway, 9th Battalion, British 6th Airborne Division

The Merville battery showing the effects of the RAF bombing.

The main force was very scattered in initial drop, with many paratroopers drowning in the flooded meadows by the river Dives. Of the seven hundred in the main force, only some 150 men had assembled by 02.30 hours. The RAF bombing took place as the troops were marching to the battery, but the bombs failed to find their true target.

Albermarles, such as this Mk. V of RAF 297 squadron based at RAF Brize Norton, were used to tow gliders and to drop 'Pathfinders' for Otway's attacking force.

If you expect that there won't be chaos, gentlemen, I can assure you there will be utter, complete chaos when you land.

Brigadier James Hill, addressing the 9th Battalion before they took off

On reaching the battery, Otway found it to be undamaged. Things got worse. The three gliders due to land against the battery arrived overhead, but Otway was unable to signal them so they landed some distance away. The Navy were to bombard the battery if they had not been told of its capture, so Otway had no choice. With too few men to surround the battery, the only option was a single, frontal attack. This involved cutting through barbed wire and crossing minefields, all under direct fire from the defenders. Amazingly, Otway's forces seized the battery and spiked the guns, but at the cost of 80 casualties in the attacking force.

So we went in and we attacked. They were taken completely by surprise, and there was hand-to-hand fighting. And I shouted before we went in, "Get in! Get in!" And one man, an officer, who shall be nameless, broke the rules by blowing a hunting horn.

Lt Colonel Terence Otway, 9th Battalion, British 6th Airborne Division

The bombing, though fierce and intense, was inaccurate, much of it falling east and south of the target. There were dire consequences for the airborne forces making their way to attack the battery. Here bombs caught a party of troops on the road and many were killed.

Battery taken as ordered Sir. Guns destroyed.

Lt Dowling reporting to Otway. Fatally wounded, he died at Otway's feet a few moments later.

Otway's signal of success – a yellow smoke candle – was seen by a Navy spotter plane and HMS Arethusa held its fire with just minutes to go. For all the bravery of its capture, ultimately the Allied intelligence assessment of the threat from Merville battery proved over-pessimistic: the feared guns turned out to be just four small Skoda 14/19 wheeled howitzers, that posed no real threat to Sword beach.

St Mère Eglise

1 Crash-landed gliders
2 Open trench air raid shelters

3 St Mère Eglise town square
4 US roadblock site

5 Site of burning barn, St Mère Eglise
6 US 101st Airborne C-47 crash site

7 US 82nd Airborne parachutes
8 Fouville village

Utah

○ St Mère Eglise

The town of St Mère Eglise, behind Utah beach and guarding access along the main road from Caen to Cherbourg (linking Carentan and the Cherbourg Peninsula) was a vital strategic objective. Securing the settlement was one of the first tasks of the US airborne forces who planned to land in six drop zones round the town before the main invasion came ashore. However, the night-time drops went badly wrong as the aircraft were driven off course by low cloud and anti-aircraft fire. As a result the troops of the US 82nd and 101st Airborne Divisions were scattered around the countryside and many had great difficulty in locating any other American soldier, let alone the men they had jumped with.

US 101st Airborne paratroopers (left) en route to the drop zone and (right) waiting for the green light to jump. An entire 'stick' of 18 men could exit the C-47 in just 12 seconds.

Troops of the 101st Airborne wait to board a C-47. A military version of the DC-3, the C-47 (also known as the Gooney Bird and the Dakota) could carry almost any kind of cargo or up to 18 paratroopers. More than 10,000 C-47s had been built by the end of the Second World War.

The crash site of a US 101st Airborne's C-47 aircraft. Struck by *flak* as it approached one of the drop zones, this aircraft went out of control and crashed into a pasture south east of St Mère Eglise. Flying at less than 1,000 feet, aircrews had little time to react to *flak* hits. There were no survivors from this crash.

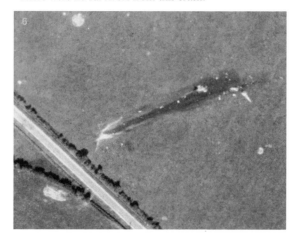

During D-Day itself a number of reconnaissance sorties were flown over the St Mère Eglise area. In the early hours low cloud hampered these inland sorties but by the middle of the day the weather had cleared. The frame on the previous page was taken by a 10th Photo Group aircraft which overflew the area at about 13.00 hours.

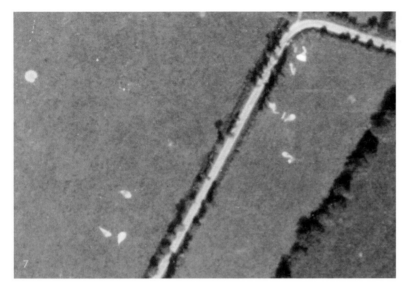

The collapsed parachutes from a stick of 82nd Airborne troopers in the fields. Elsewhere clusters of collapsed parachute canopies may be seen from similar sticks dropped nearby.

Famously, the barn in St Mère Eglise which burned down on the night of June 5th-6th. It was the breaking of the curfew here by the villagers, who formed a bucket chain to put out the blaze, that led to the German garrison being in the town square when 101st Airborne paratroops landed across the town. Thirteen paratroopers were killed in this action, which was one of the earliest clashes of D-Day.

St Mère Eglise town square. A stick of the 82nd Airborne dropped into this square as the residents fought the barn fire. The paratroopers fell into trees, the square, and in the case of the US 505th's Parachute Infantry Regiment's Private John Steele, onto the church steeple itself. Steele's escapade (he was shot and captured, but later escaped) became part of the book and film 'The Longest Day'.

'... it was kind of shocking to see these little fields that we had to try to land in. But we didn't have much time to think, as we came in at about 800 to 1000 feet at the most…so I decided on a nice ride across fields and hedgerows, until I finally lost my lift. I picked this one spot in a hedgerow that didn't look like it was too solid and headed for that, and that's where we crashed.'

Robert Jeep, US Glider Pilot 436th Troop Carrier Group

In the pre-dawn hours of June 6th, US paratroopers were reinforced by 102 gliders carrying heavy equipment such as jeeps and guns. But many of the Pathfinders who were to mark the landing zones were themselves lost. Few places could be correctly marked in time, and almost no gliders landed in their designated areas. Casualties among the glider-borne troops and crews were high amid the trees and tall hedgerows. Here two gliders have crash-landed, one in an orchard, another in a hedgerow. Brigadier General Donald Pratt of the 101st Airborne division was killed in just such a crash-landing.

On the morning of June 6th a US jeep towing an anti-tank gun, and approaching St Mère Eglise from the direction of Chef du Pont (after landing by glider), struck a mine at a roadblock laid by US paratroops. The jeep, the gun and the roadblock were destroyed and the two occupants of the jeep were killed. This is the site of that roadblock.

A typical US forces Jeep, with machine gun.

Overall the night-time parachute and glider landing by the US 82nd and 101st Airborne Divisions had gone badly, with heavy casualties and troops and equipment widely scattered. Nevertheless, at least one objective was achieved. By 05.00 hours on D-Day, Colonel Edward Krause of the US 505th Parachute Infantry Regiment had fulfilled his promise to have the Stars and Stripes flying from the St Mère Eglise town hall. The town had been secured.

Eighteen men of the US 82nd Airborne Division lie dead after their Horsa glider crashes in Normandy; June 6th 1944.

Air attacks in the Cotentin Peninsula prior to D-Day led the Germans to create zig-zag shaped open trench air raid shelters. These were used as defensive positions during D-Day and during the fighting inland from the beaches.

Fouville village. During D-Day itself German occupied Fouville village formed the southern perimeter of the US-held area round St Mère Eglise. A German attempt to by-pass St Mère Eglise from Fouville was thwarted by US forces.

St Marie du Mont and The Band of Brothers

1 Deployed parachutes of 101st Airborne
2 St Marie du Mont church tower
3 Brècourt Manor

4 105mm guns concealed in a hedgerow
5 Tanks and lorries exit Utah beach

Easy Company of the US 506th Parachute Infantry Regiment, 101st Airborne Division, were tasked with seizing the town of St Marie du Mont, capturing the garrison and securing the landward end of Causeway E2 off Utah beach. Their drop was typical: the Company was scattered over 12 miles of French countryside and their Commanding Officer (CO) was killed when his plane was shot down. Lt Dick Winters of Easy Company came down near St Mère Eglise and was faced with a four mile hike towards St Marie du Mont in the pre-dawn darkness and confusion.

St Marie du Mont church tower. At dawn on D-Day, German Commander Frederick von der Heydte climbed this tower to gain his first view of the US forces approaching Utah beach. Stunned by what he saw, he dashed north to a hidden gun battery at Brècourt Manor, but found it deserted, so he continued back to Carentan to secure troops and artillerymen to bring the Brècourt guns into action against the landings at Utah.

The only thing I had when I hit was the maps that were in my pocket, and a jump knife that was strapped to my leg. That's all I had. So that's a heck of a way to start a war... laying behind in Normandy, on D-Day, no weapons, scattered all over the place. This is a great way to start a war!

Dick Winters, US 506th Parachute Infantry Regiment, 101st Airborne Division

Deployed parachutes of a stick of US 101st Airborne personnel. Note how close together the individual parachutes are. Dropped at low altitude – often less than 1,000 feet, these paratroopers all landed within a few seconds of each other.

During the night, Easy Company joined up with other elements of the 2nd Battalion. At around 07.15 hours on D-Day morning, the Battalion came across the battery of four 105mm guns near Brècourt Manor. Not only had these been missed by Allied photo intelligence, they had just gone into action – firing at Utah beach.

Brècourt Manor. Seat of the Vallavieille family, the Manor was used by the Germans as the headquarters for their gun battery to the north of the Manor. Footpaths from the Manor to the battery are evident, but the Bigot map of the area missed the gun positions themselves.

At approx 08.00 hours, thirteen men of Easy Company, led by Dick Winters, were dispatched to seize the Brècourt guns, which were now held by a 50-man platoon of German paratroopers. This action was later immortalized in the book and film 'Band of Brothers'. In a three hour battle Easy Company managed to destroy three of the guns, and with five reinforcements from D Company also destroyed the fourth. The gun crews were scattered and most of the defending German paratroopers killed, wounded or captured, before the US soldiers withdrew under heavy machine gun fire from near Brècourt Manor. Pale marks in the open ground in front of the gun positions indicate impacts from grenades thrown by Easy Company.

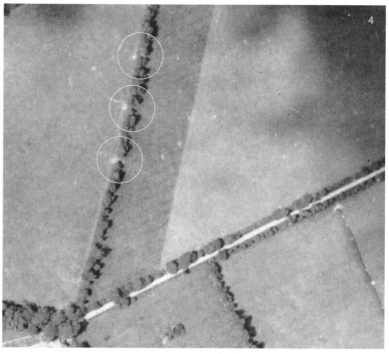

Three 105mm guns concealed in hedgerow north of Brècourt Manor. They began firing on the invasion fleet and Utah beach, and would also threaten US forces pressing inland along the causeways from Utah. Slight breaks in the hedgerow indicate the position of three of the guns. The fourth lies off the top of the picture. A thin pale line against the hedge indicates the footpath the crews took to reach the guns.

Vehicles from Utah beach Exit 1 advancing towards St Marie du Mont. It is likely that the Sherman tanks seen here were those diverted a few minutes later by Dick Winters to help attack the German machine gun positions at Brècourt Manor, which was finally secured by mid-afternoon.

Utah Beach

1 Attacked fortifications close to shore
2 US 9th Air Force bombing
3 The strong point at Les Dunes de Varreville
4 Le Mesnil strong point
5 The strong point of La Madeleine
6 Amphibious DD Sherman tanks arrive on the beach
7 Le Chalet Rouge
8 *Wiederstandnest 5*
9 US troops taking cover on Utah beach
10 Landing craft leaving the beaches
11 Attacked fortifications behind the beachhead

The earliest images of Utah were taken by two reconnaissance aircraft which took off at 06.00 hours from Mount Farm. The new 7th Photo Group Commanding Officer, Norris Hartwell and his deputy, Lt Colonel Clarance Schoop were determined to witness D-Day unfolding for themselves. These images are from the sortie flown by Hartwell.

Utah Panorama

'H-Hour' was the moment at each beach when the first wave of soldiers would go ashore. At Utah H-Hour was to be 06.30 hours and by that time the heavily mined, but otherwise undefended Isles St. Marcouf were seized and secured. However, smoke, dust and the lack of three of the four primary control craft resulted in the landings going astray. The main force was displaced 2,000 yards southwards along the coast, with the Tare Green beach force actually landing on Uncle Red, and the Uncle Red force on Victor. Just before the assault, US 9th Air Force aircraft bombed the coastal fortifications. The first wave force consisted of some 1,200 men, and amphibious Duplex Drive (DD) tanks of the 70th tank battalion landed at 06.50, some 10 minutes after the first troops arrived.

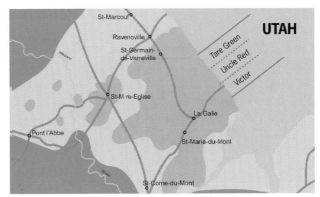

US 9th Air Force bombers have attacked gun positions and other fortifications behind the beachheads (right) and also close to the shore (below). Unlike at Omaha, US bombing has actually been carried out on the beach itself, providing shelter that was to prove sorely lacking on that beach.

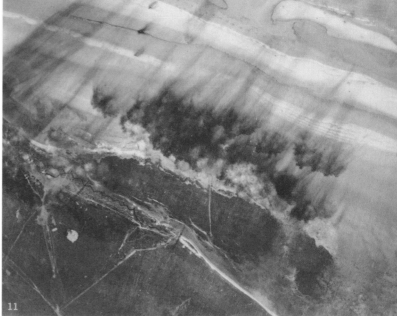

The strong point of La Madeleine. One of the more fiercely defended German positions, La Madeleine controls access along an important lateral track behind the Utah beachhead.

A B-26B Marauder of 397th Bomber Group, US 9th Air Force. B-26s of the 397th bombed the Utah beach fortifications, including those at La Madeleine, just ahead of the beach landings on D-Day. Flying at low level and in the face of heavy anti-aircraft fire, bombing at Utah was an unqualified success. This photograph was taken in August 1944 and shows off the rather worn black and white invasion identification stripes found on almost all Allied aircraft that flew in support of D-Day.

They took us to an assembly area where we went around in circles until all the other people who were making the invasion were there. I'll never forget that sound. We didn't know when we were going in, but when they revved up the motors – that sound comes back to me many times in my life, at the funniest times – I'll remember that sound as long as I live. Because now we're going in.

Leo Jereb, staff sergeant US 4th Division

A Landing Craft Infantry (LCI) loaded at Dartmouth, England; June 1st 1944. LCIs were capable of carrying around 200 troops. Their task was to deliver these troops directly onto the beaches through the forward ramp, then pull back off the beach and go back out to sea.

Landing craft leaving the beaches. In comparison with the approach to Omaha beach, US landings at Utah were relatively lightly opposed. Later, the gun batteries inland will bring the beaches under shell fire, and they remain in range of German guns for several more days.

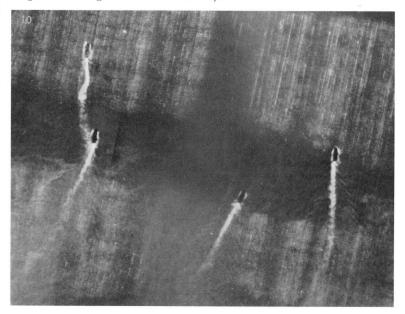

LCI stands for Landing Craft Infantry. But sailors have a slang name for everything, and we always said it stood for "Lousy Civilian Idea". And that's like the larger landing ships, the LSTs: really their proper name was Landing Ship Tank, but we called them "Low... Slow, Targets."

Elmer Carmichael, Bosun Mate US Coast Guard

A Landing Ship Tank (LST) seen here loaded with trucks in preparation for D-Day. Flat bottomed, the LST was designed to off-load its cargo of trucks or tanks directly onto the beaches.

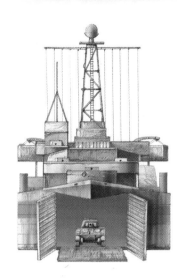

An LST with its bow doors open and ramp lowered. Here it is loading an army field kitchen.

Three plan views of a Landing Ship Tank (LST).

Many of the American troops have landed in the wrong place and overall the troops are displaced about a mile south of the intended landing areas. General Roosevelt consults with Colonel Van Fleet about the possibility of moving the force back towards the intended landing areas. At about the time these images were taken, General Roosevelt (according to legend) declares, 'We'll start the war right here.'

On Omaha beach troops were exposed to concentrated fire from the defenders and lacking bomb craters, the attackers were continually exposed. Bomb craters on the beach at Utah provide shelter for some, and the resistance here is lighter than elsewhere. Here US troops can be seen taking cover on the beach itself.

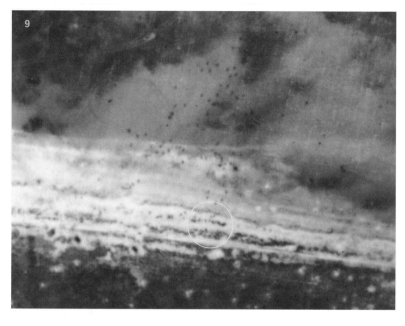

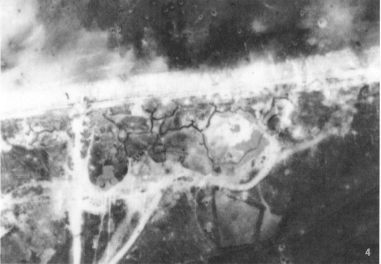

The German strong point at Le Mesnil. One of three strong points on the Utah beach stretch, this position will be overcome within a few hours.

When the ramp went down, that's when I remember all the noise; and when that ramp went down, I asked myself, "What am I doing here?". But I was about to find out in a few minutes what I was there for. I jumped into the water with my rifle over my head and I waded through the water, it was about chest-high. And when I reached the sand, I just ran as fast as I could to the top of that knoll and burrowed myself into that sand.

Leo Jereb, Staff Sergeant US 4th Division

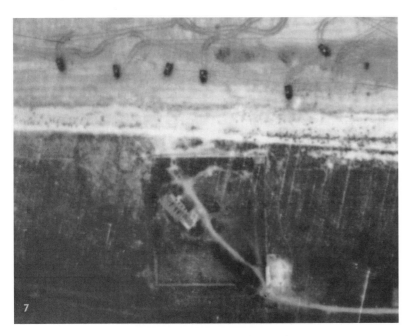

Bombing by the US 9th Air Force was generally effective at Utah. Here a complex of farm buildings has been hit and set on fire by the aerial bombardment. Civilian casualties in the beach areas are surprisingly low.

Le Chalet Rouge. This house in its compound lies on the northern edge of *Wiederstandnest* (WN) 5. Behind it lies Exit 2 running towards St Marie du Mont.

Wiederstandnest 5 at La Grand Dune, fronting Causeway E2. The road here divides Utah beach sectors Uncle Red on the left and Victor on the right. Opposition from the strong point is not preventing tanks of C Company, US 70th Tank Battallion making their way onto the causeway which is threatened by guns sited inland at Brecourt manor.

This strong point at Les Dunes de Varreville (STP 9) was one of several under construction by the German coastal forces during the months of April-May 1944. In the event, none of these strong points will withstand the American assault for very long.

A DUKW amphibious vehicle. Universally known as the 'Duck', the DUKW was a development of the General Motors two-and-a-half ton truck. The floating truck was designed to help troops bring ammunition, food and supplies of every sort ashore without the need to off-load at the sea's edge from a landing craft. The Duck could sail out to sea, load up from the heavy transport ships, bring the cargo ashore and then, turning into a truck, it could drive up the beach and onto the roads to deliver its load several miles inland. More than 2,000 Ducks were used on D-Day to carry every imaginable load ashore. Until the giant Mulberry docks were constructed along the Normandy beaches, the Ducks are estimated to have carried about 40% of the daily average of 14,500 tons of supplies ashore.

Amphibious Duplex Drive (DD) Sherman tanks arrive on the beach. These tanks, an invention of British General Hobart, are making their way up the beach towards the network of trackways giving access to the causewayed exits beyond.

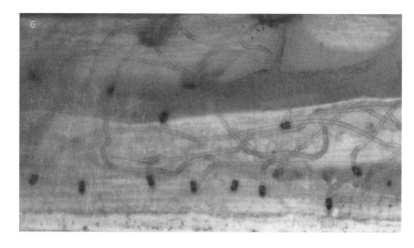

Hundreds of ships of all sizes and shapes, from vast battleships to small barges, littered the surface of the sea. Some were still completing their rough passage across the Channel, others lay at anchor while the big men o' war belched forth sixteen inch shells from their gun turrets in the direction of the French countryside; two Seafire fighters buzzed above the battleships like flies around a cart horse, spotting the accuracy of the gunners below and supplying them with corrections.

Sleek destroyers guarded the flanks of the shipping armada, while overhead patrolled the ever-watchful fighter cover.

Minesweepers plied their steady patrol back and forth, and an occasional column of water rose to prove the value of their efforts.

Superimposed on this fantastic picture were the ghostly outlines, in my mind, of the pathetic little fleet that I had watched standing off the beaches of Dunkirk. The pendulum had gone full swing. A feeling of savage delight passed through me. "Right, you bastards," I thought, "you've asked for it and now you're going to get it." There was no mercy in my heart. Our Spitfires swept past the moored fleet and commenced the vigil over the two American beaches of Omaha and Utah.

Geoffrey Page, Flight Commander, RAF 122 Squadron

The M10 Tank Destroyer was a 76mm gun mounted on a Sherman chassis – in essence a powerful gun but with less protection than a standard tank. Manned by a crew of five, the M10s (also known to the British as the 'Wolverine') saw action throughout Normandy.

The 'Priest' was a 105mm howitzer gun mounted on a medium tank chassis. Above the howitzer is a 0.50 machine gun. Priests were used by artillery units to support tanks.

Used to transport infantry, the 'Halftrack' was a truck with tracks at the rear, and wheels at the front. It had some protective shielding and various weapons could be mounted in the rear compartment.

Pointe du Hoc

Pointe du Hoc

On the morning of D-Day, Pointe du Hoc was to be attacked by men of the US 2nd Ranger Battalion arriving in several Landing Craft Assault (LCAs). Part of the force were to arrive at the base of the cliffs and the main force was to come ashore at the Vierville draw on the western edge of Omaha beach, and work its way inland to attack Pointe du Hoc from the land side. In the event, only a small part of the force reached the base of the cliffs, nearly 40 minutes late, and they were faced with climbing the sheer cliffs of Pointe du Hoc while under determined fire from the German defenders.

During the sea approach only three LCA's (861, 862, and 888) arrive in the correct place. Navigational errors lead to the main force being deployed through Omaha beach, and being unable to reach Pointe du Hoc in time for the assault.

Pointe du Hoc

Grandcamps-les-Bains

1 Guns concealed in orchard
2 Profile of Pointe du Hoc cliffs
3 Lt James Eikner's signalling point

Photographed by a 10th PG F-5, the Rangers are holding their positions at Pointe du Hoc nearly 48 hours after the invasion. When this image is taken, at last, reinforcements are just about to arrive.

Anyhow, we arrived 38 minutes late, and the Germans were up on the top side waiting on the ship and at us coming in…The boys didn't mind going up and down the cliffs, even with a pack on. But when they're shooting at you, it's a little more difficult.

I said, "Boys, they're throwing grenades. Turn your faces in and your butts out." If you got to get some shrapnel, your butt, you could handle that shrapnel a lot better than your face…

I looked up there, and here is this German soldier leaning over the cliff. He had his chin in his hand, leaning over. And I looked around for my tommy-gun. It was not too far away, but out down in the mud. I pulled it out, and he was still standing there. I said, "Well, you bastard," and I raised it up and 'click'. It wouldn't fire. My gun was clogged up with mud. And I thought to myself, "Ain't this a hell of a note? Here I am in the damnest war in history, and with no gun!" Now why that German up there didn't shoot me, I don't know – he could have very easily; he could have picked me off.

James Eikner, 2nd Ranger Battalion

The first command post to be set up is at Pointe Du Hoc. Ruder's Rangers are in the bomb damaged ruins of a German bunker on the cliff edge. It is from here that Eikner signals 'Praise the Lord' indicating that the Rangers are up the cliff.

Pointe du Hoc in the first light of D-Day. The aerial and naval bombardments here, the most recent ending just before this image was taken, have been a success. The concrete gun emplacements have been hit and three of the guns had been damaged. On June 3rd, the day before the second air attack, the guns had been removed from the batteries and concealed further inland in an orchard south of the Grandcamp – Vierville road; a fact which French resistance chief Jean Marion was keen to report to London.

Men from LCA 888 scale the cliff within 15 minutes of landing. The near-vertical imagery shows the Pointe during the assault by Ruders' Rangers. At this time the team from LCA 861 are engaged in a fierce firefight with the German Observation Point (OP) while Rangers from LCA 862 are doing the same from the other side. Other soldiers are beginning to work their way south towards the gun positions, which they will find unoccupied, the guns having been moved back three days earlier.

The orchard where the guns are concealed. The Rangers will push southwards to over-run and destroy the guns in their temporary concealment. After further bitter fighting they also find and destroy a large store of munitions. The guns were ranged on the stretch of coast which was very shortly to become Utah beach. Had it not been put out of action, the battery at Pointe du Hoc battery would certainly have inflicted severe casualties there.

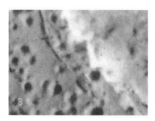

The approximate spot where 1st Lt James Eikner and other Rangers scaled the 90 foot high cliffs and set up the first Command Post.

The fall of the shadows here shows the distinctive profile of the cliffs of the Pointe du Hoc.

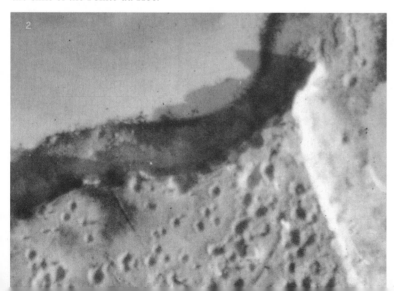

Omaha Beach

These first images of Omaha beach were taken by Lt Col Clarance Schoop in F-5B 42-67382 at approximately 06.45 hours, i.e. H-Hour +15. Patches of low cloud cover the beach and so instead of making a continuous pass, Schoop opts for short photo 'legs' where he can see activity. Those locations are the four draws (valleys) from the beach, and the surrounding areas. This resulting mosaic, though of variable quality, catches the beach at its earliest and deadliest moments.

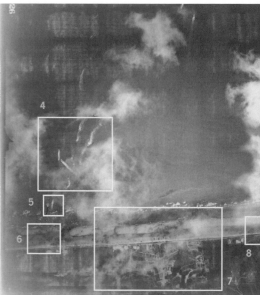

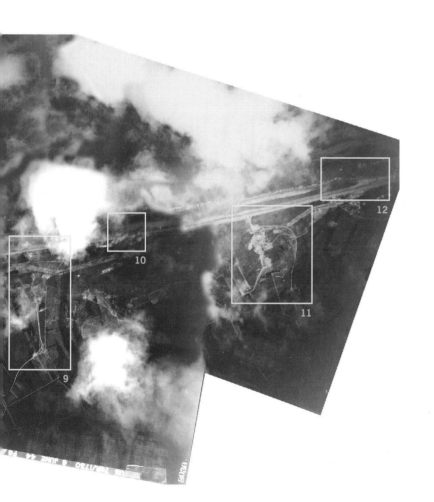

Omaha Panorama

The invasion plan at Omaha was for a naval bombardment at 05.50 hours to soften up the German defenders. From six miles out to sea the USS Texas, Arkansas, Nevada, Tuscaloosa, Quincy and Black Prince would pound the shore batteries. The naval bombardment would be followed by US 8th Air Force bombing at 06.15 hours and 15 minutes later, at H-Hour (06.30), the first amphibious DD tanks would come ashore, having been released several miles out to sea.

Low cloud led to fears that the bombing might kill Allied forces through 'creepback' and so the bomb line moved inland, making the aerial effort less effective. Then the amphibious tanks planned to be the first forces ashore became casualties: half were not launched because the seas were too rough while the remainder were released between 7 and 9 miles offshore, where most sank. At H-Hour the rest of the two Tank Brigades were to be put ashore, to take on those coastal strong points not destroyed by Naval shelling and Air Force bombing. But the German defenders were battle-hardened veterans from the Eastern front and were far from destroyed. From bunkers and strongholds flanking the beach exits they poured a withering fire onto the first waves of infantry, which inflicted heavy casualties on the attackers and threatened the whole beachhead.

USS Nevada. Launched in 1914 she saw service in the Atlantic during the first World War and was badly damaged at Pearl Harbor in 1941, before being repaired to support the D-Day landings,

The USS Nevada with its 14 inch guns was perhaps the most powerful ship attached to US Forces. Here she fires a salvo at German gun positions inland from the beachhead.

The Vierville Draw. One of the designated exits where the German resistance is at its fiercest; WN 72, right on the beach, pours fire into the attackers who are pinned down. Soldiers instead force their way inland between the designated exits. Brigadier-General 'Dutch' Norman Cota and Colonel Canham land between Draws D1 and Draw 3. By 09.00 they will reach the top of the bluffs and push west and east to take the German positions flanking the Vierville, and Les Moulins draws.

Wiederstandnest 72 in action on Exit D1. From their bunker at the end of the approach road to the beach, German forces hold US troops at bay for several hours.

The sectors of Omaha beach.

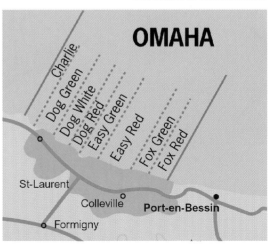

OMAHA

Charlie
Dog Green
Dog White
Dog Red
Easy Green
Easy Red
Fox Green
Fox Red

St-Laurent

Colleville **Port-en-Bessin**

Formigny

Here 'Life' magazine war correspondent Robert Capa is taking some of the most dramatic D-Day photographs of all with his Contax camera. Landed at about this time with the first wave, Capa instinctively records the bloody scene before him. Evacuated later in the morning on an LCI, Capa reaches London in the evening with three rolls of film – only to have all but eleven frames of them ruined in the darkroom.

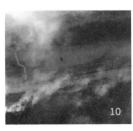

A dramatic Coast Guard photograph of a smoke-trailing Landing Craft Vehicle Personnel (LCVP), known as a Higgins boat, making for the shore at Omaha. The boat was hit by gunfire which exploded a grenade. The craft made the shore and landed its men.

An early shot showing infantrymen wading shore from their Higgins boat on Easy Red. Directly in front of them is a DD tank, one of few to make it ashore at this early hour. It is thought this one was from Company A of the 741st Tank Batallion.

Here Higgins boats are landing troops of the 16th Infantry Regiment under fire on Easy Red. Troops can be seen moving forward past obstacles shortly to be covered by the still rising tide. Drifting smoke obscured the German view of some beach areas but provided scant protection.

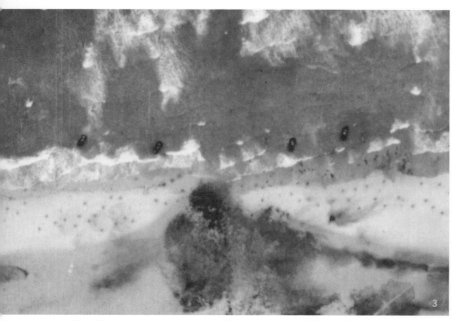

The Higgins boats in which the first waves of the US 16th Division are landing. The German defenders, however, are waiting for them and the US troops will be cut to pieces during the initial hour.

On the run-in to Omaha beach soon after H-Hour. US troops crouch well down from the sides of the Higgins boat, though the man at the port bow is keeping vigilant lookout. In minutes they will hit Easy beach.

And when that ramp went down, the Captain went off first, and by the time he hit the end of the runway, he was full of bullets. The machine-guns just opened up, they had us in a crossfire from two different guns up in the cliffs. And when he reached the end of the ramp, he just fell over in the water. And two other men went off – one of them was a friend of mine, my Sergeant at the time – he went off, he was hit. I was the fourth man, and that sea was rough. And somehow I hooked my heel or tripped or something in the excitement of being scared to death – this was the first time I'd ever been under fire, this was the first time anybody had tried to kill me – and I fell off the side and I went straight to the bottom.

Robert Sales, 116th Infantry Regiment, 29th Infantry Division

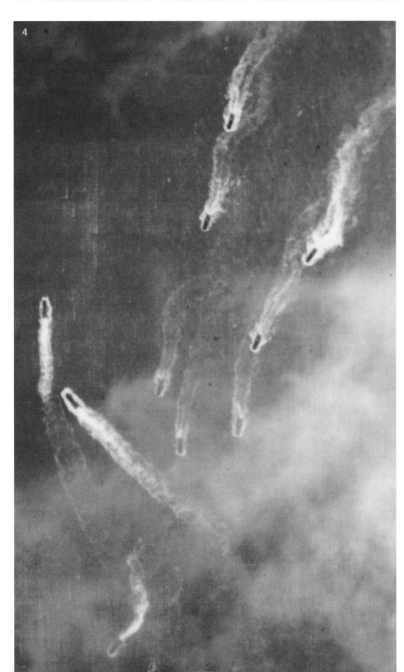

4

Incoming craft off Dog White. The first wave of landing craft have rapidly foundered, but reinforcements continue to come in. Here eight LCAs are approaching the beach while two others withdraw.

Easy Red beach. Here is LCI 553 which hit a pole-mounted mine off Draw E3 and had to be abandoned. To its right, in front of the bows of another craft, can be seen a beachside villa marking Draw E1. Drifting smoke hides the beach from WN 62.

When we beached the first time, I was up front on the bow, and I could see very well, and you could see the froth, the red froth right at the water's edge. And all of a sudden it dawned on me that it was blood from our soldiers that's in the water, and it's kind of frightening.

Elmer Carmichael, Bosun Mate US Coast Guard

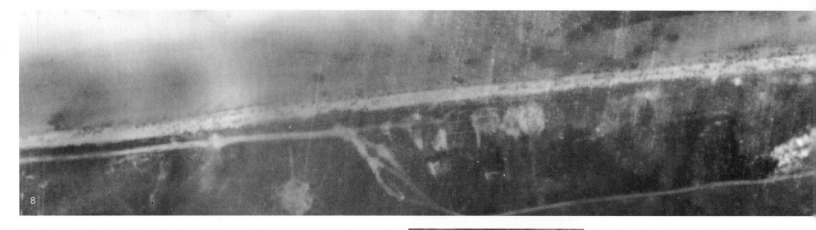

The German fire from the main draws is intense. Here groups of soldiers can be seen huddled against the shingle bank and the sea wall on Easy Red. The first troops off the beach climb up the bluffs here and between D1 and D3 to attack the German positions from the land side.

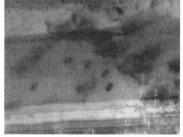

The first DD tanks have been launched between six and nine miles offshore, and very few of them make it to the beach in the rough seas. Their absence is crucial at this earliest, critical stage in the attack.

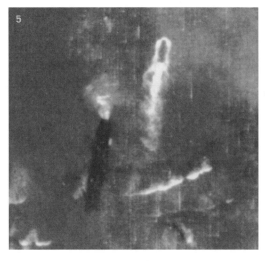

A Landing Ship Tank (LST). Losses to the amphibious DD tanks launched out to sea have been appallingly high, and the bulk of the tanks which will have any effect on this day will be landed from LST's such as this one.

Les Moulins draw (Draw 3) is the division between Dog Red and Easy Green. The difficulties in getting inland up the draws are immense, and troops remain pinned down in this vicinity by four *Wiederstandnesten* (WN) – two flanking the draw itself, and two further inland (WN 67 and 69).

Omaha beach as seen from about 500 yards inland from Draw E1 soon after the invasion. This is a German gunner's view of US shipping at anchor off the beach.

Exit E3. *Wiederstandnest* 62 on the west flank of Fox Green beach. Traditionally this is the point where the first US troops touch down at 06.20 hours, ten minutes before H-Hour. In a short time, elements of the US 16th and 116th Infantry Regimental Combat Teams (RCTs) are to land here 'inside a series of very well prepared killing areas'.

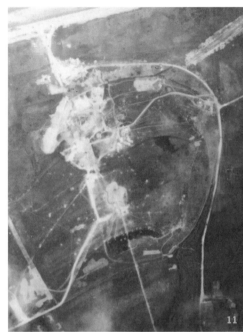

WN 64. Flanking exit E1 on Easy Red beach, this strong point, with WN 65, will hold US Forces at bay until 2nd Lt John Spaulding of Company 'E' 16th Regimental Combat Teams (RCTs) with a team of men manages to get inland and attack the position from the rear. That battle will lead to 21 prisoners being taken. During late morning Engineers force an access over the anti-tank ditch and create an important exit off Omaha, Draw E1.

Fox Red and Draw F1. I and L Companies US 3rd BLT landed here. This is the eastern most sector of Omaha beach, where the beach itself narrows and the bluffs, defended by WN 60, immediately rise up. Company L will shortly land here and begin their fight to liberate Europe. Company I is still making, in error, for Port en Bessin.

1 USAF bombing
2 DD tanks
3 A US destroyer off the beach
4 3rd Company 743rd Tank Battalion
5 Engineering Battalion Sherman tanks
6 Major Bingham's strong point
7 Troops on the beachead

8 Bulldozers at work
9 Landing Craft Infantry 1552
10 *Wiederstandnest* 60
11 USAF bombing

This mosaic is created from imagery taken by an F5 Lightning at about 13.30 hours. The tide is now high. Everything is hanging in the balance.

Later Omaha

Seeing disaster unfolding, US Navy ships respond by moving in as closely as possible, supporting the few DD tanks which have made it to the beach by engaging the German gun positions. The morning fighting is bitter as troops press ashore between the exits. Conflicting messages record the confusion. At mid-day General Bradley, on USS Augusta considers diverting follow-up force 'B' to Utah and Sword beaches, while the defending German 352nd Infantry Division reports that the American forces have been thrown back into the Channel.

I lay there on the beach and was trying to decide when to go across, and I could still see the machine-gun tracer bullets, firing across, and you could hear the firing, and the tide was coming in real fast…

I keep running and running and running and running – it seemed like forever – and I got to the sea wall, and I was out of breath and I was scared to death. And here comes Williams and Algary right behind me. So I don't have a weapon; they don't have any weapons. So I take my assault jacket off and I spread my raincoat, and I start to break my rifle down to clean it, and there was bullet holes all in my assault jacket and my raincoat. Well, I tried to light a cigarette, and my hands were shaking so bad – and my matches were wet – I couldn't get my cigarette lit. And I was just shaking real bad. I had to finally compose myself, and I just kept saying to myself, "Get a hold of yourself. You got to do this, you got to do it."

Bob Slaughter, 116th Infantry Regiment, 29th Infantry Division

A Landing Ship Tank (LST) lands its cargo of US 3rd Company 743rd Tank Battalion DD Sherman tanks which are making their way along the beachside track. The first two Tank Battalion Companies, due to come ashore at H-Hour, had been launched six to nine miles out to sea and many foundered. The third wave, landed at the beach edge, are more fortunate. Lack of tanks is still a major problem for the US forces pinned down on the beach.

Omaha beach Draw E1 soon after June 6th, showing shipping protected by on-board anti-aircraft guns and close-hauled balloons to deter low-level air attack. Later the balloons were dispensed with altogether.

Engineering Battalion Blade-equipped Sherman tank. The drivers of these vehicles have one of the most important, and unenviable, tasks – cutting access routes across the sea wall at the western end of the beach, and through the shingle so troops can get to the beach exits. Bulldozer drivers will win two Distinguished Service Medals this day.

Taken in clearer weather during the late morning this image shows US 1st Division troops disembarking on a falling tide. Vehicles and gun towing half-tracks are moving along the beach as soldiers are making their way up the slopes of the bluffs. While nearby German defences have been largely eliminated they are still active, soon after taking this picture the photographer was hit and wounded.

Bulldozer hard at work at Draw E1. This image catches it during the earliest, most dangerous phase in their work. A war correspondent remembers them under fire, pushing their way through to the roads.

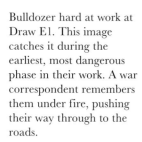

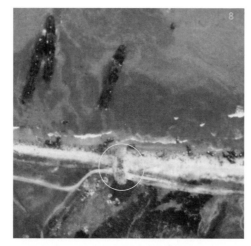

Omaha beach. Troops taking temporary shelter in the shallows on Easy beach behind tetrahedral and three DD tanks from the 741st Tank battalion. Few of these amphibious tanks made it to the shore in the early morning and those that did provided infantry with what little cover there was.

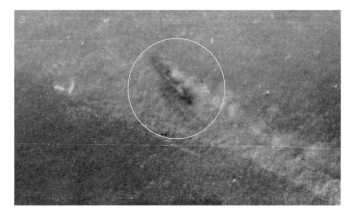

A US destroyer off the beach. During the morning the Navy have come in as close as they can to support those Sherman tanks which have made it to the beach, despatching the gun positions at Draw D1, D3, and here, at Fox Red. At the end of the day General Gerow signals Bradley 'Thank God for the US Navy'.

Major Sidney Bingham's strong point. During D-Day morning Battalion Commander Sidney Bingham with 50 'F' company men have taken control of this three-storey seaside Villa and made it the temporary control point of the 16th Infantry Battalion. From here Bingham launches an attack with ten men on WN 66 in the bluffs above.

When I laid on that dune line, a sailor that was on our assault boat lay down beside me. I said, "How old are you?" He said, "I'm 17." I said, "What the hell are you doing here?"

Michael Accordino, Private First Class, 299th Engineer Combat Battalion

Landing Craft Infantry 1552 lies abandoned on the shoreline after striking a mine during the run-in to the shore.

The beachhead opposite WN 65 protecting Draw E1. With the tide still close to full, the beach is narrow and heaving with men and machines all under fire.

They were supposed to bomb the beach. They didn't bomb the beach, and the reason for that is because it was too cloudy from the smoke, they were afraid that they would hit the troops, our troops. So there were no craters on the beach. They said there would be craters on the beach for us to crawl into if we had to, and there were none on the beach. So that was a big problem there.

Michael Accordino, Private First Class, 299th Engineer Combat Battalion

A formation of B-17 Flying Fortresses of US 709th Bomber Squadron, 447th Bomber Group.

USAF bombing. Here and elsewhere on the main panorama can be seen the scattered effects of the bombing delivered at 06.15 hours by the US 8th Air Force. Poor visibility and low cloud has led to the bomber force, not wishing to bomb the landing troops, waiting until they are clearly over land. The result is that the bombs have done little to disrupt the coastal fortifications, which quickly went to action stations when the bombing ceased.

DD Tanks on shore moving towards exit D1.

Stationed off Omaha, the USS Augusta – Admiral Kirk's flagship – was also General Bradley's D-Day HQ. Here the ship fires a salvo at a German position with its eight inch guns. As the bridgehead hung in the balance, Augusta closed to less than two miles off the beach to support the US troops.

US success is signalled by Vth Corps which sends a message to General Bradley on Augusta, 'Troops formerly pinned down on beaches Easy Red, Easy Green, Fox Red advancing up the heights behind beaches'. Slowly the US forces silence the gun positions flanking the draws and begin to move inland.

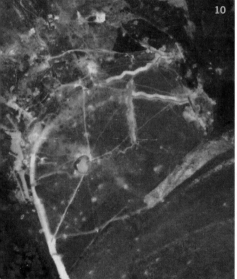

WN 60. This is the position from which the commander of *I Abteilung Artillerie* Regiment 352, Major Werner Pluskat, reported sighting the Invasion Fleet to 352 Division HQ. In what – thanks to Cornelius Ryan (author of *The Longest Day*) – will become one of the best-known exchanges of the war, Division HQ asks Pluskat 'Where are these ships heading?' 'Right for me' he replies.

Bombing. US 8th Air Force bombing south of the coastal defences has only churned up open countryside. Later aerial bombardment against communications routes, isolating Normandy from the French rail network and later against concentrations of German armour is to prove more effective.

I was the only survivor... there were 30 men on board that boat, and I was the only man to get off alive.

Robert Sales, 116th Infantry Regiment, 29th Infantry Division

1 Bomb craters
2 Exit route Lane 1
3 Jig Green beach
4 AVRE's attempting to bridge a blocked road
5 Jig King sectors of Gold beach
6 Jig King beach boundary
7 Minefields

8 Mont Fleury Battery
9 Lavatory Pan farm
10 *Wiederstandnest* 34

These images of Gold beach are taken at about 12.00 hours by Lt Cameron Captain of the US 7th Photo Group flying sortie 7/1743.

Gold

Some 6 miles to the east of Omaha beach lay the British beach Gold, stretching from Arromanches to La Riviere. H-Hour here would be 07.30 hours – an hour later than at the American beaches as low tide came later here than to the west. This gave the British attackers an advantage in that the air and sea bombardment would last longer before the troops came ashore. However, they would do so in broad daylight.

Gold was designated to the British 50th (Northumbrian) Division, including the 1st Dorset, 1st Hampshire, 6th Green Howard and 5th East Yorkshire Regiments and the 47th Royal Marine Commandos. Although the German strong points are more thinly distributed here than at Omaha, the beach and underwater obstacles

(hedgehogs, stakes and tetrahedra) are more numerous than anywhere else in Normandy. They are also larger and more effective than the attackers are expecting. These obstacles are even more dangerous as the strong northwesterly wind is bringing the sea in higher than normal – even at low tide – and many of the obstacles are unseen under the water's surface.

Immediately behind the beaches there are more villages and towns than at the American beaches. Although in some sectors the attackers can expect to break through into open countryside which is less flooded or protected by tall hedgerows than elsewhere, in other sectors they will have to take on the enemy in house-to-house fighting.

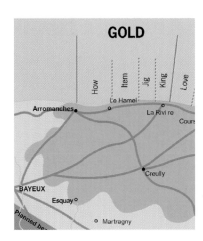

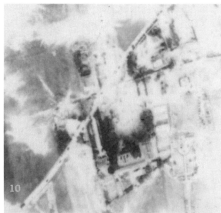

Inland from Gold are a number of important strong points including this at Mont Fleury – WN 34 close to Mont fleury battery. This strong point surrounds a lighthouse and is the objective of the 5th East Yorkshire Regiment after they have eliminated the La Rivière fortifications. Although bombed, little damage has been caused.

Bombing here, as at Omaha and Utah, has been a precursor to the attack. On Gold, bomb craters occasionally make the exits off the beaches impassable, creating bottlenecks and traffic jams. These long lines of vehicles present sitting targets to any Luftwaffe aircraft that can reach them – only Allied air superiority will offer any real protection.

'Lavatory Pan' farm (so-called because of the shape of the twin approach drives). Here during the morning Company Sergeant Major (CSM) Hollis has charged and subdued two German pillboxes single-handed, taking 25-30 prisoners. Later he will go on to subdue gun positions in Crepon village. For this act he will later be awarded the only VC (Victoria Cross) to be won on D-Day itself.

Just east of Le Hamel, the road dividing Item and Jig beaches is blocked by a crater. This exit route, designated Lane 1, is the objective of Assault Vehicle Royal Engineers (AVREs) of the 82nd Assault Squadron and the Hampshire Regiment. Only by evening was Le Hamel and its fortifications overcome.

Mont Fleury Battery, where the Germans have completed two of four casemates. Heavily bombed by 4th Group RAF Bomber Command, during the aerial attack just before H-Hour, Major Anderson reports later that the target has been 'well hit…The main weight…fell on the emplacement and on the auxiliary buildings'. Had the 122mm gun been put out of action? He said it appeared to have fired off all its ammunition.

A lateral road has been blocked by a bomb crater. AVRE's are attempting to bridge the crater with a Small Box Girder (SBG) bridge to allow traffic to flow off the beach. Delays caused by road blocks of this kind are substantial. The AVRE is one of the specially modified vehicles invented by General Hobart, known universally as 'Hobart's Funnies'. These specialized vehicles are used to great effect on the British and Canadian beaches.

Sherman 'Crab' Mine-Clearing Flail. Seen here mounted on a Sherman tank, the Crab (also known as the Scorpion) used a forward-mounted flail to clear a path through minefields by setting off the mines well ahead of the tank itself. forty chains were mounted onto a drum that revolved under power from the main tank engine. Further developments included wire-cutting discs and a flail that could follow surface contours and so be more effective over rough ground. The Crab had regular Sherman armament and could be used in a combat role.

Mk IV Churchill Tank. After a poor experience during the Dieppe raid of 1942, the Churchill was not fully introduced into service with the British army until 1943. With earlier reliability problems overcome, the Churchill proved itself adept at handling uneven ground and was developed into many specialized versions, including flamethrower, bridge layer and the Assault Vehicle Royal Engineer – AVRE.

Churchill AVRE. Based on the Churchill tank, various versions of the Assault Vehicle Royal Engineer (AVRE) saw service on the British and Canadian beaches during D-Day. The AVRE was designed to have various attachments fitted – including frames carrying demolition charges, bulldozer blades and – as seen here – track-laying equipment. AVREs were also fitted with a mortar for demolishing obstructions and fortifications. AVREs remained in service with the British Army until the 1960s and the concept is still in use on current British tanks.

A late morning vertical aerial photo of Gold beach near Le Hamel, 'the Dart' showing the inland advance of the 1st Dorset Regiment. This area has been subjected to a heavy naval bombardment as can be seen by the numerous craters in the fields. All landing craft have left the beach area and the tanks are now moving inland. A large column of vehicles has formed on the road and successfully bridged the damaged road section in the center of the photo.

A vertical image from the same sortie slightly further along Gold beach, showing the landing of the 6th Green Howard Regiment and the 5th East Yorkshire Regiment at La Rivière. This area has been heavily shelled and the main road along the top of the beach has been damaged making it difficult for the tanks to move along it. Tanks can be seen on this road and on the beach along with beached and partially submerged landing craft. A few fully laden landing craft are coming into the shore. The large oblique white line across the center of the photo is a German anti-tank trench system with a set of anti-glider stakes running across the trench.

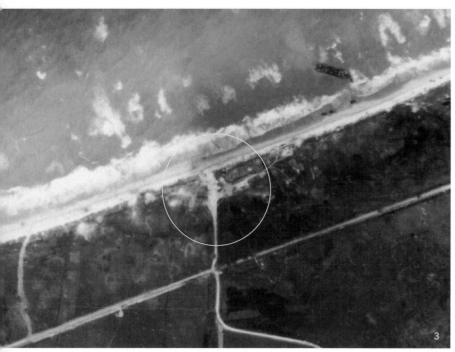

Jig Green beach. Just west of here, three AVRE Lane Clearance Teams (LCT's) are to be landed to create exits off the beach between Le Hamel, 'the Dart' so named from air photography – and WN 36, in front of Le Roquettes. In the event these teams all land further east than intended where they find little evidence of aerial bombardment. The Hampshires, slated to storm the Dart, are landed here instead, securing this strong point which was the intended target of the 1st Dorset Regiment.

The Jig-King beach sector boundary has a road running inland. By about 08.20 hours the assault on the beach is over and access to these important inland routes is forced. Armoured traffic is quick to use the route to penetrate west of the Mont Fleury Battery in the direction of Ver sur Mer, which is a primary objective of the Green Howards. Here a line of armoured vehicles can be seen pushing inland.

Inland from the beaches with their mine-tipped underwater defences are numerous minefields. Photographic reconnaissance was surprisingly successful in detecting these as grass grew rapidly in wired off areas where cattle could not graze. Mines buried at shallow depth killed off or parched the grass growing above them and became visible from the air. Here rows of white specks indicate the position of land and anti-tank mines which were plotted on the Allied intelligence maps well before D-Day.

Viewed around the time of maximum congestion when the tide was at its height on D-Day morning are the Jig-King sectors of Juno - the area attacked by the 50th Northumbrian Division. To the west of the dividing road, on Jig Red is the area of the 1st Dorset Regiment with, on King, the Green Howards designated area, King Red.

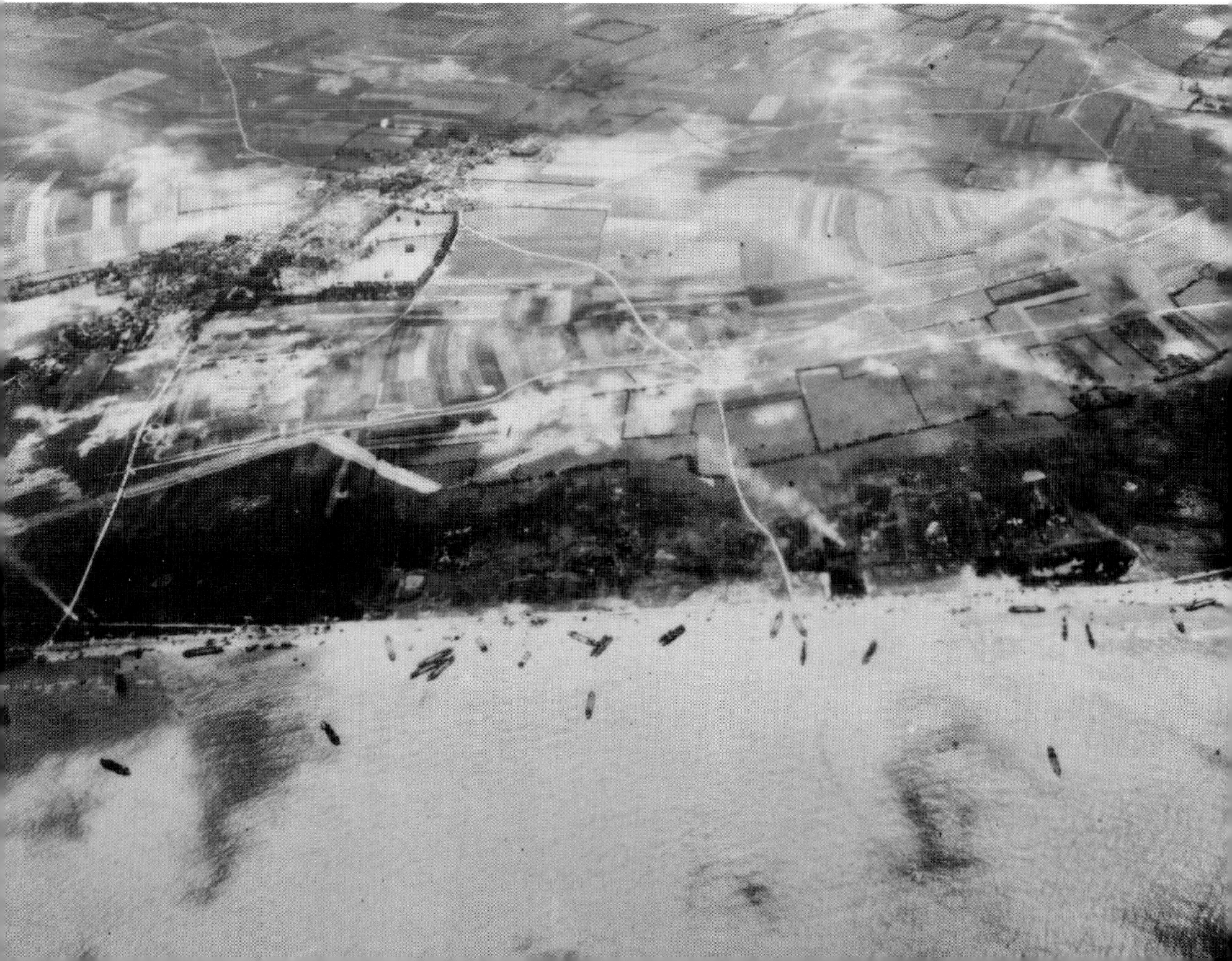

An oblique photo of Gold during late morning on D-Day showing the landing of the 50th Northumbrian Division. Naval bombardment has set fire to the vegetation in the surrounding fields forming isolated plumes of smoke. Tanks and landing craft litter the beach and many more landing craft are coming ashore with more equipment. A column of tanks can be seen moving off the beach to the right of the photo in an attempt to move inland.

1 Exit Mike 2
2 *Wiederstandnest* 31
3 Courseulles sur Mer
4 *Wiederstandnest* 29

Captain Hubert Childress took these images during a sortie that lifted off at about 12.50 hours.

Juno

After the disaster of the 1942 Dieppe raid, where a full three-quarters of the attacking forces (predominantly Canadian) were killed, wounded or captured; the Canadian attackers were eager to prove and avenge themselves on D-Day.

Allocated a stretch of coast that included Courseulles – the most heavily defended point between Arromanches and Ouistreham – the Canadians faced a number of villages and small towns strung out along the beach that might have to be taken in hand-to-hand fighting. Supported by the 48th Royal Marine Commandos, the 7th and 8th Brigades of the Canadian 3rd Division also had the objective of linking up with the British forces coming ashore to the east at Sword beach. The gap between these beaches would offer the ideal striking point for a German counter-attack that could push the Canadian and British lines back before they had a chance to link-up.

H-Hour was scheduled as 07.45 hours, and as at other beaches an aerial bombardment took place – both by the RAF during the night June 5th – 6th and at dawn on June 6th by the US Air Force. As at Omaha, the bombing was not accurate and most if not all the fortifications were left intact. Also in common with other beaches, the amphibious DD tanks were often late to arrive, having struggled to 'swim' fast enough to stay ahead of the landing craft carrying the first wave of infantry.

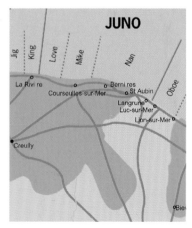

8TH CANADIAN B
LANDING RN

7ᵀᴴ CANADIAN BDE.
ᴰING AT COURSEULLES
970858

A low-level oblique photograph taken at late morning on D-Day. The 8th Canadian Brigade are landing at Bernières sur Mer to the left with the 7th Canadian Brigade landing at Courseulles. Naval shelling has set alight buildings in the town and vegetation outside in the fields shown by smoke plumes. Note how windy it is by the low angle of the smoke plumes. As with the other beaches rough seas have led to many DD tanks foundering. The rising tide, narrowing the beach, has also led to heavy casualties in equipment and men. The LCAs can beach but have difficulty getting off.

'We swept parallel to the coast beneath a leaden sky, and I positioned the wing two or three hundred yards off-shore. Our patrol line ended over the fishing village of Port-en-Bessin, while further to the west, beyond our area of responsibility, lay the two American assault beaches… As I watched the Naval bombardment I realized that we flew constantly in airspace between the Naval gunners and their targets. No doubt the shells were well above our height of 2000 feet, but I made quite certain that we did not exceed this altitude.

Here and there the enemy appeared to be putting up a stiff resistance: we saw frequent bursts of mortar and machine gun fire directed against our troops and equipment on the beaches. Small parties of men could be seen making their way to the beach huts and houses on the sea front, many of which were on fire. But the greatest danger to us pilots lay from the mass of Allied aircraft which roamed restlessly to and fro over the assault areas. Medium bombers, light bombers, fighter-bombers, fighters, reconnaissance, artillery and naval aircraft swamped the limited airspace below cloud – on two occasions we had to swerve violently to avoid head on collisions.

'Johnnie' Johnson; Wing Leader 144 Canadian Wing, 83rd Group 2nd Tactical Air Force

Exit Mike 2 (M2) is blocked by bombing which has destroyed the bridge,
A tank trap in front has been widened by a shell crater to around 60 feet
– too wide to be bridged, and a Churchill tank carrying a fascine has
been lost into the shell hole. Using great ingenuity, the turret of the
sunken tank is used as a pier and two 30 foot bridges are laid across the
gap by bridge-carrying tanks. Thus by 09.15 a temporary causeway has
been created. By the early afternoon, after further improvements, M2 is
open and traffic is passing over the causeway. This 'temporary' bridge
will remain in use until the sunken AVRE tank is recovered in 1976.

Aerial bombing has left the German position WN 31 undamaged and here, in
the words of their War Diary, B and D Companies of the Winnipeg Rifles
'…had to storm their positions cold'. With the assistance of the tanks which put
the positions out of action, B Company captures the beach pillboxes, crosses the
bridge over the Seulles and clears the approach to the port.

Just west of WN 29 east of the river Seulles. This strong point too is undamaged by bombing and here DD tanks from B Squadron of the British 6th Armoured Regiment appear to have been responsible for silencing the guns with extremely accurate fire from close range, as reported by the Special Observer Party which inspected the bunkers later.

Western suburb of Courseulles sur Mer. This important port has been divided into 12 zones for the assault. During the attacks about 80 enemy prisoners have been taken, and the town has been secured by the attackers at about this time. The general view is that the town was more strongly defended than had been suggested by Allied intelligence.

I do not remember how many missions we flew to the Orne Estuary: for these missions, our planes carried bombs under the wings. Our losses during these attacks on the Allied bridgeheads were enormous. I had seen how my comrades were butchered. These combats were so cruel, and the enemy's air superiority so overwhelming that we were pulled out of action after a few days, having suffered about 75% losses.

Aegidius Berzborn, III/*Zerstorergeschwader* 1

One of the June casualties, a III/*ZG* 1 Junkers 88 after crash landing behind German lines.

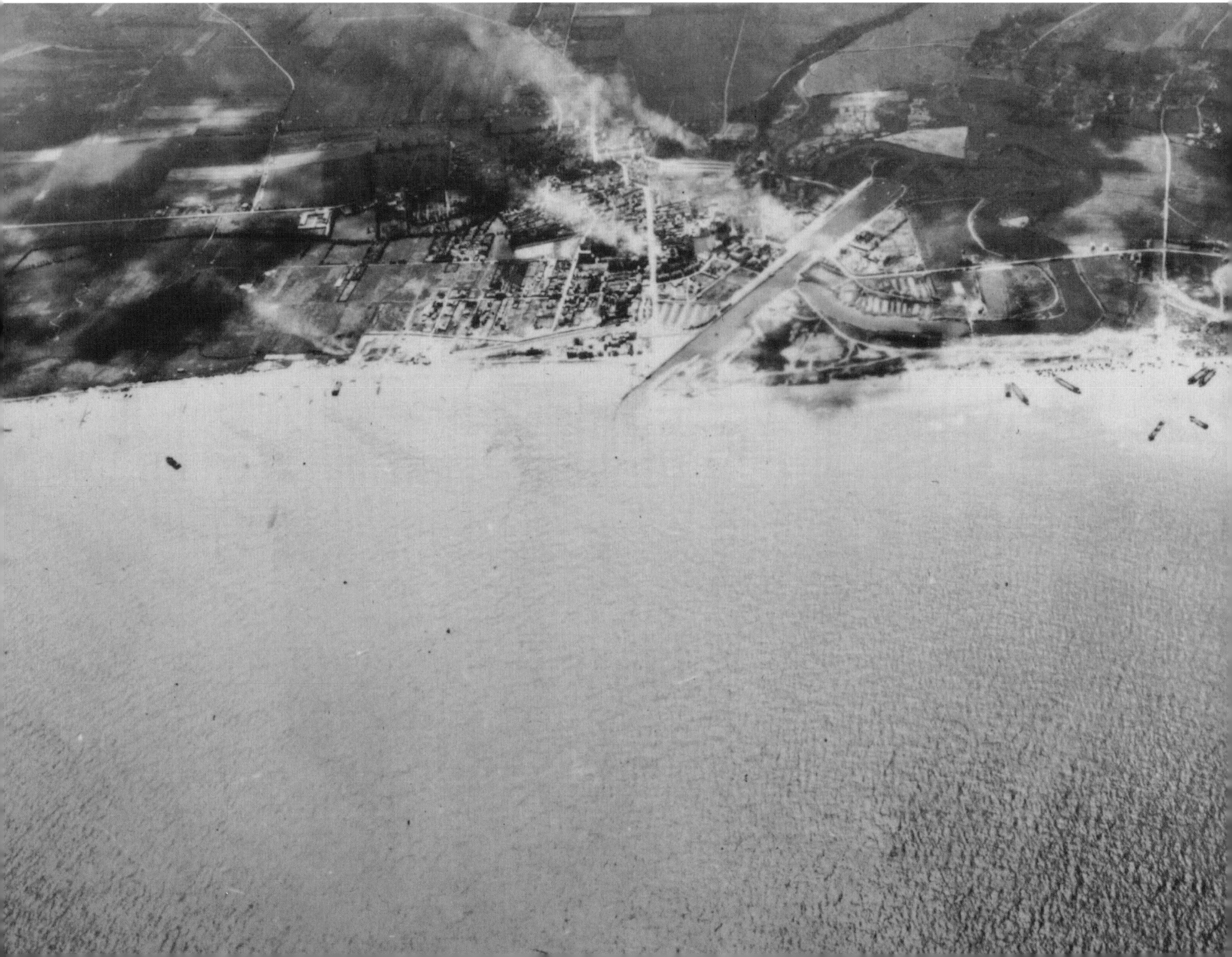

A low-level oblique photo on the late morning of D-Day looking at Courseulles on Juno beach. Landing craft can be seen high up on the beach with other craft coming in to supply more troops and equipment. At the entrance to the two main roads off the beach, center right, troops and vehicles can be seen massing and starting to move inland.

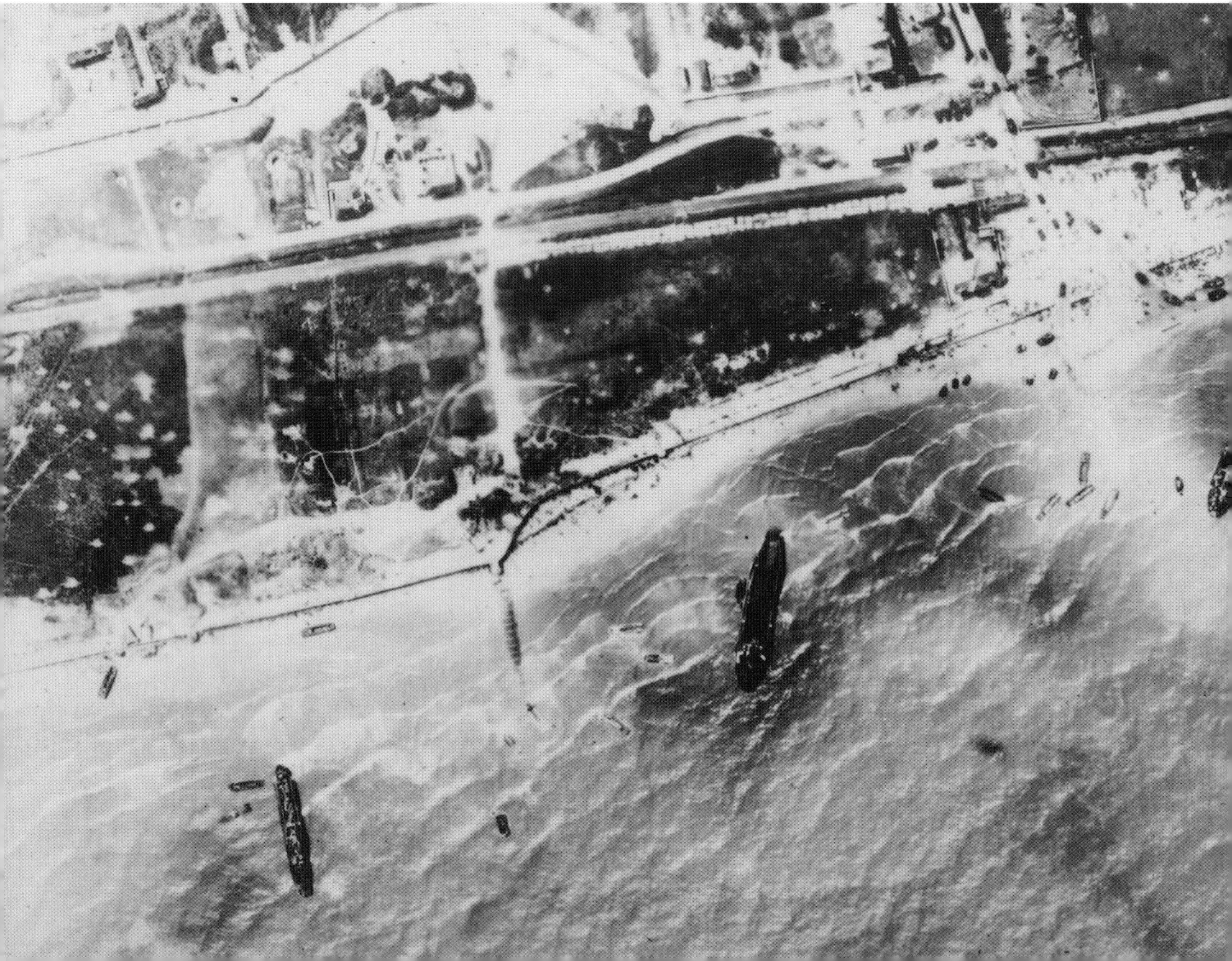

A vertical aerial photo taken late morning over the town of Bernières sur Mer on Juno beach, showing the inland advance of the Canadian 8th Brigade. Large tank carrying landing craft (LCTs) are on the beach with their doors down and empty whilst others are queuing to get on to the beach. Smaller troop carrying landing craft (LCIs) lie beached or destroyed in the shallow waters. Tanks, jeeps and troops are massed along the high part of the beach and can be seen moving inland via the two main roads.

A late morning photo of part of the Canadian 8th Brigade at La Rivière on Juno beach. The white craters in the fields surrounding the town show that this area has been subjected to intense naval bombardment. A few tanks and trucks remain on the beach whilst advanced units of tanks of the Canadian 8th Brigade have set up defensive positions in the fields just inland. By late morning on the June 6th, all fighting on Juno has ceased and troops are free to begin their journey inland.

A vertical aerial photo from the late morning sortie showing the progress off the beach at Exit M2 of the 7th Canadian Brigade just west of Courseulles. Two partially sunken landing craft lie in the shallow waters to the left of the photo. Two LCTs are on the beach and have discharged their load, a third is coming in to offload – tanks and other large mechanized equipment can be seen on its decks. Tanks and troops are just moving off the beach along the only road in this section.

At the other end of Juno beach on Nan Green beach to the east of Courseulles, other detachments of the 7th Canadian Brigade have landed and moved off the beach. In this photo there is little evidence of tanks or troops at this time. Bridges have already been built across the anti-tank ditch backing WN 29 in the middle of the photo, enabling the rapid advance inland of troops and vehicles.

The D-Day planners realized early on that the success of the invasion would rely not only upon getting men ashore but also in getting tanks on to the beaches – to clear obstacles for the assault troops and to help establish a bridgehead. Several experiments were tried with tanks of the 79th Armoured Division under General Sir Percy Hobart, known as 'Hobart's funnies'. Giant canvas screens were erected above the tracks of 32 ton Sherman tanks to give them buoyancy. These DD (Double Duplex) tanks could then be steered ashore and once on the beach the canvas screen would be thrown off and the Sherman could go straight into battle.

This system worked well in calm seas but unfortunately on the morning of D-Day the weather was anything but calm and many of the swimming tanks were launched too far out in choppy seas – with the result that many sank straight to the bottom. There were also bulldozer tanks and tanks with rotating flails attached to clear minefields. The British led the experimental use of tanks but the Americans were less convinced of their value. On the British beaches the tanks played a vital role in the success of the landings but on Omaha beach 29 out of 32 tanks sank on launching and the infantry were left to fend for themselves amongst the beach obstacles and under intense fire from well prepared defensive positions.

1 *Wiederstandnest 20A*
2 Eastern end of Queen beach
3 *Wiederstandnest 20*
4 La Breche
5 *Stutzpunkt* Riva Bella
6 Ouistreham
7 Franceville Plage

This panoramic image was created from Sortie 7/1734, which was flown by Captain John R Hoover. The tide is high and there is very little beach area at this time. The aircraft seems to have been flying over the beachhead at about 09.45 hours.

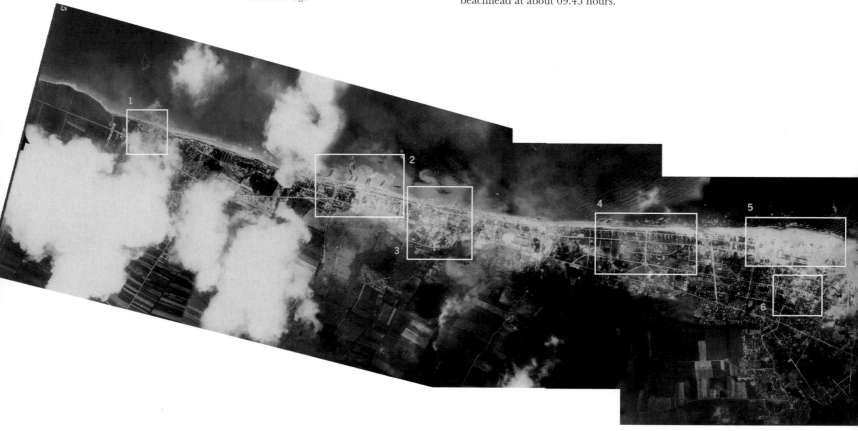

Sword

Sword was the easternmost of the beachheads selected for the Normandy landings, stretching from Lion-sur-Mer to Ouistreham. These landings put the attackers closest to the ambitious objective that Montgomery had set the British army – namely the capture of the city of Caen, some eight miles inland from the coast. They also put the landing forces under the guns of the gun batteries at Merville and Le Havre. Merville was disabled before dawn by British airborne forces led by Lt Colonel Otway, and the guns at Le Havre were engaged on D-Day morning by HMS Warspite, in an action that drew their fire away from the beaches. Also with the British forces were elements of De Gaulle's Free French commandos, who now, at last, could return to, and fight for, their homeland.

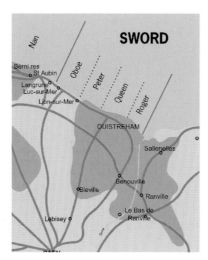

HMS Warspite. Completed in 1916, HMS Warspite had already been severely damaged twice in the Second World War during action off Crete and Italy, and was partially repaired to cover the D-Day landings. On June 6th HMS Warspite attacked the guns at La Havre, which could threaten Sword. She was further damaged a few days after D-Day by a mine off the English port of Harwich.

Under fire on Red Beach soon after landing James Mapham took this image of unidentified troops and Beach Group personnel taking shelter. There are casualties in the group.

Press photographer James Mapham of the Leicester Mercury took these images as he approached Sword beach at about 08.00 hours on June 6th. The rising tide has still to cover the tetrahedral ahead. On the beach a DD tank burns.

Strong point WN20 (Allied code 'Cod' or strong point, 0880) on the edge of Queen White and Queen Red beaches. It contains an estimated 20 positions including machine guns, two anti-tank guns and mortars and was to be captured by the East Yorkshire and the South Lancashire regiments. It took three hours to take the area and casualties were 'heavy'.

WN20A, which is to be captured by 41 Royal Marine Commando, lies nearly a mile from the closest landing point. 41 Commando are to go on to meet 48 Commando from St Aubin (coming from Juno beachhead).

It was inevitable that Ouistreham, one of the few towns on a designated invasion beach, would suffer damage from the bombing of the Riva Bella battery. Here craters from misses can be seen among the villas and blocks of the little port.

Here, as elsewhere, the rising tide has created severe congestion on the beach, but once the beach exits are cleared, vehicles can penetrate inland rapidly. Within a couple of hours of the H-Hour (07.45 hours), Hermanville – about a mile and a half inland – falls to the British forces.

At the extreme eastern end of Queen beach, the 1st Special Service Brigade is to land and push inland. First to land is 4 Commando which includes Free French troops, whose objective is a battery and garrison in Ouistreham, the *Stutzpunkt* Riva Bella.

Those looking for national stereotypes would find plenty of material at Sword. One British colonel allegedly read Shakespeare to his men on the run-in to the beach; Lord Lovat's personal piper marched up and down the beach playing the bagpipes. Almost every soldier seemed to have brought a bicycle along. There was also a heavy reliance on clever gadgets: the first wave was guided ashore by midget submarines that had lain just offshore for some 48 hours. As well as the amphibious DD tanks there were many other 'Hobart's Funnies' on hand – flame throwers, bridge layers, flails to clear a path through minefields and so on.

But for all the impression of a Sunday outing, the British forces would come ashore right in front of heavily defended positions including pillboxes, fortified villas and houses right at the edge of the beach and, although they did not know it at the time, they would also be within easy striking distance of the tanks of the German 21st Panzer Group – if they were mobilized quickly enough.

Perhaps the best known of the British D-Day images is this iconic shot, taken by a professional photographer Jimmy Mapham on White beach looking towards Red beach showing different troop formations including Royal Army Medical Corps (RAMC) personnel tending wounded, and 8th Brigade Troops.

Lane 4, one of the tracks off the beach just to the east of strong point 0880, was one of numerous routes off the beach established on D-Day. Here mesh is being set down to give vehicles sufficient grip to get off the beach without bogging own in the soft sand. Note the Sherman flail in the background. Behind, troops disembark from LCI's.

A Sherman flail tank lies bogged down on the sand of Sword beach. Flails, one of Hobart's 'funnies', proved their worth time and again in the first hours of D-Day.

The sea front villas and plots on the western margins of Ouistreham were given the code name Oslo on the Bigot intelligence maps. The road running at right angles to the beach separates Roger Green and Roger White beaches. While the beach is relatively quiet, the area behind is being traversed by the Free French and the 8th Infantry Brigade for the assault on the guns at Riva Bella near Ouistreham casino.

Perhaps the most formidable strong point on the entire Sword beach sector is *Stutzpunkt* Riva Bella. Under construction here are positions for six 155mm guns which could wreak havoc on the incoming naval vessels. These positions are to be attacked by the 171 Free French Commandos under Colonel Phillippe Kieffer. Naval bombardment has struck and put out of action the uncompleted rangefinder building (which will remain occupied by some 50 Germans until June 9th). At 09.25 hours, following a bombardment from a Centaur tank, the position was taken. The storming of this position is an epic feat of arms the French justly celebrate.

A frame from the film taken by Captain Evans. This shows Commandos under the command of Lord Lovat going ashore at H+1 hour. The figure on the right is piper Bill Millin, who struck up 'Blue Bonnets' as he disembarked. The figure to his left in the water is identified as Lord Lovat. The Commandos did not wear steel helmets, preferring berets instead.

Franceville Plage. The position of the gun position on the opposite bank of the Orne river can be clearly seen in his enlargement. Had the position been completed by the time D-Day happened it could have wrought untold damage on the Allied naval units off Sword beach. It was left unbombed.

Chest high in water, holding their kit at shoulder height, troops wade ashore on a rising tide from an LCI, which is raising its ramps before backing out to sea. Only a fortunate few made it to the land dry-shod.

View of the British Invasion fleet off Sword Beach on June 11th. A view taken through a 650mm telephoto lens from the opposite side of the river Orne in front of Franceville Plage, by German *Kriegsberichter Leutnant* Hans Ertl. It shows the mass of Allied shipping plying back and forth with supplies for the expanding beachhead.

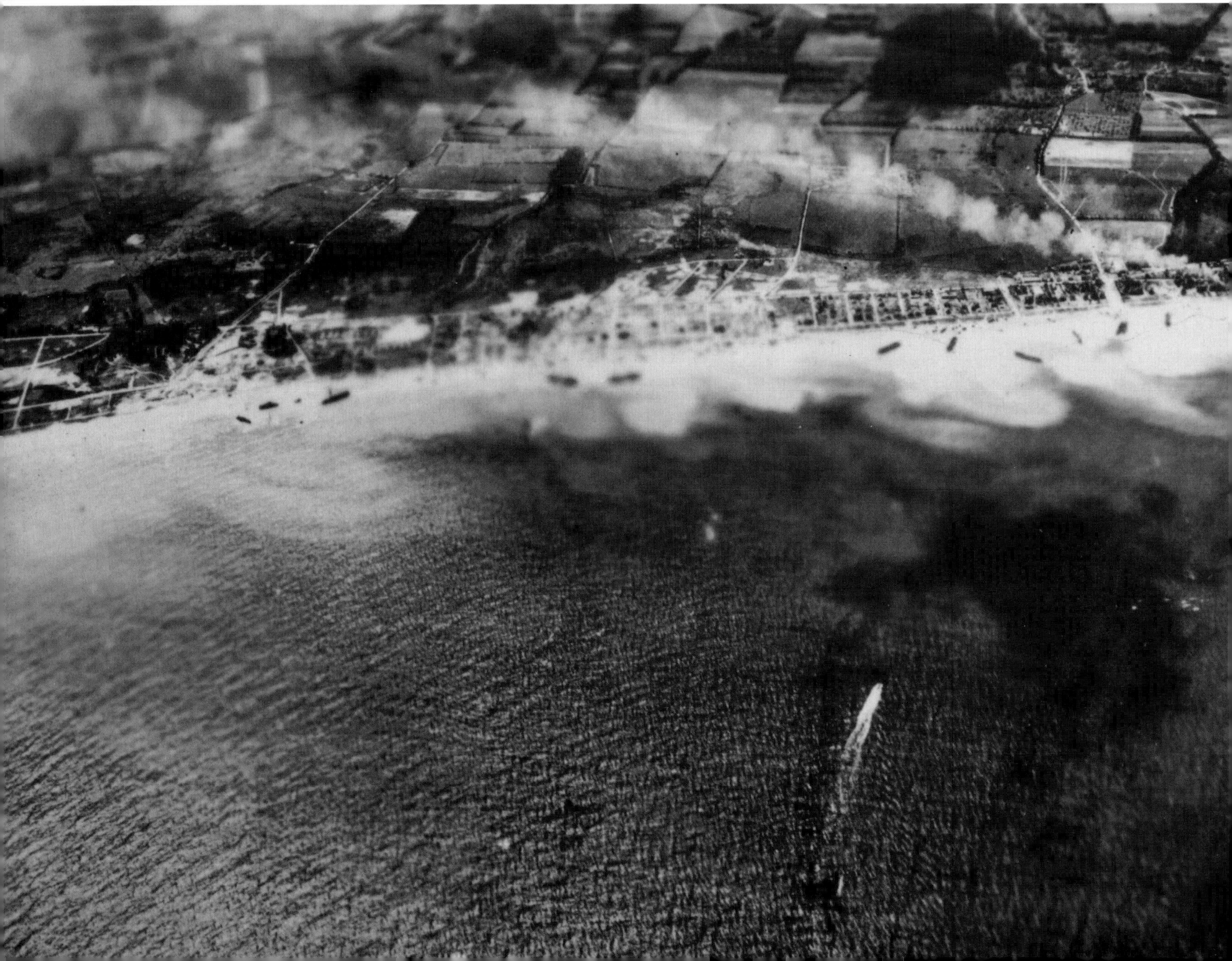

A low angle oblique photo of Sword beach late morning June 6th. The attacks are finishing on the main beach and troops were preparing to move inland. The beach area shows the town of La Bréche to the right, an array of landing craft strewn across the narrow beach and one additional landing craft heading in shore at the bottom of the photo. Smoke can be seen coming from the burning houses at the edge of the town.

Sword beach towards late afternoon June 6th, showing the aftermath of the landing of the 2nd East Yorkshire and 1st South Lancashire regiments at La Bréche. Note the large area of beach now exposed by the receding tide. Many landing craft are beached and numerous tank tracks can be seen across the beach. All the landing craft are empty, troops and vehicles can be seen at the top of the beach and on the roads preparing to move inland. This section of the beach and inland of the beach shows evidence of heavy naval bombardment as shown by the numerous white impact craters.

Beyond D-Day

Tugs pull a section of prefabricated Mulberry through the English Channel.

Supply

The Allied forces did not plan to secure any port in the D-Day landings – they did not want troops to be occupied in an expensive fight which would only win them dynamited installations and wrecked quaysides. Nevertheless, some sort of sheltered anchorage was going to be needed in the days after D-Day to bring troops and equipment ashore. The ingenious answer to this problem was to take an anchorage to France. Within days sheltered water was to be created off all the invasion beaches by the creation of breakwaters made up of sunken ships. These were called 'Gooseberries'.

At two places there were to be much larger facilities. Within four days of the D-Day landings, blockships were sunk at these locations to create sheltered water, and ten days later the ready-made ports were to be established in their final form. In great secrecy, elements of a substantial port were constructed and towed across the Channel to be sunk in pre-determined positions. Each facility would be the size of Dover Port in England (almost opposite Calais). A US Mulberry (Mulberry A) was to be constructed off Easy sector at Omaha beach, and a British Mulberry (Mulberry B) was to be built off Gold beach at Arromanches. They were intended to have a short life, three months at most, after which it was anticipated that captured ports such as Cherbourg would be pressed into service and take over. In the event, a summer storm which began on June 19th wrecked Mulberry A in its half completed state. With Cherbourg about to fall it was decided not to replace it and parts were used in the final construction of Mulberry B. Mulberry B was the port through which the Allied beachhead was supplied and was used until the end of 1944. During this period an estimated 2.5 million troops and 500,000 vehicles came ashore here.

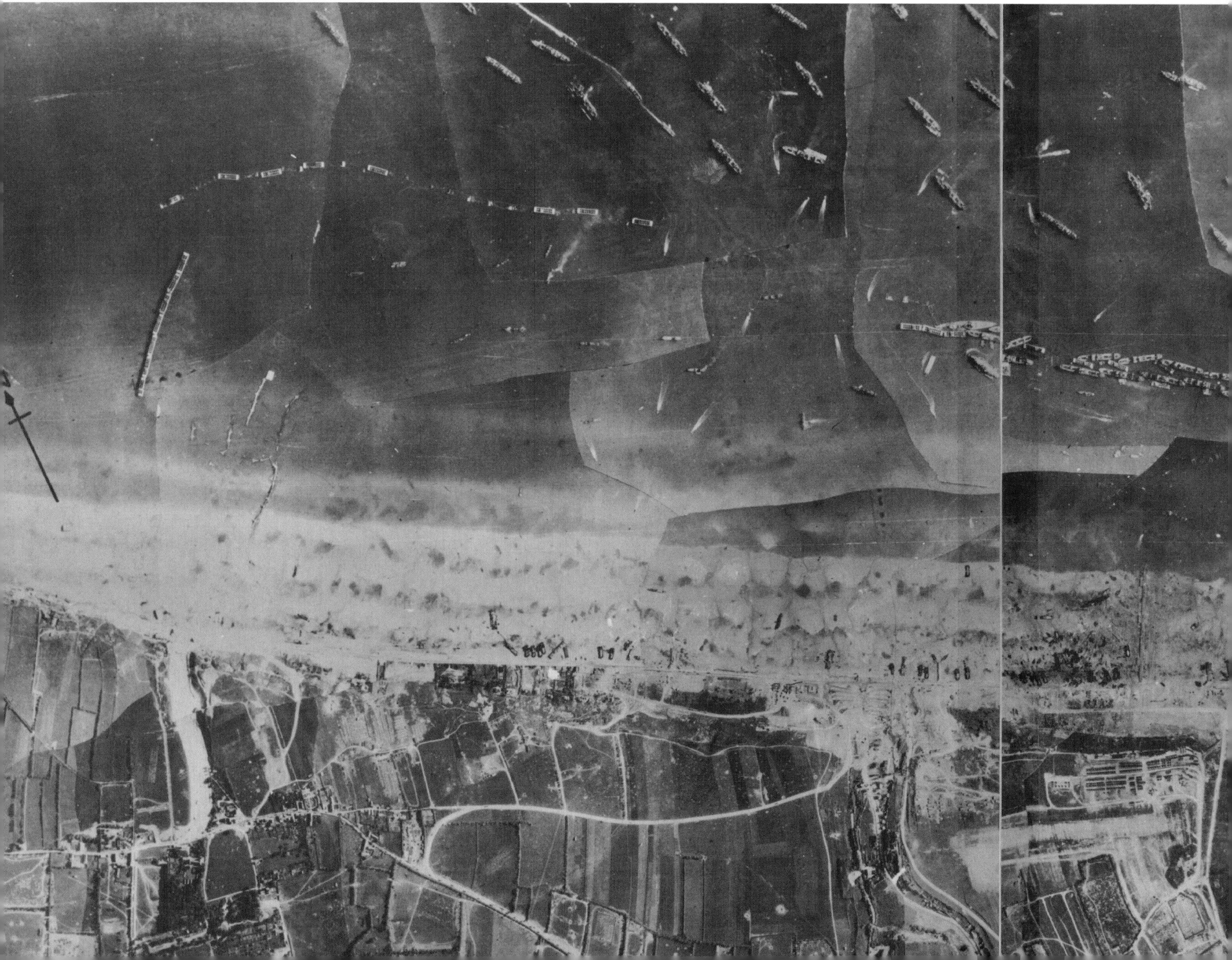

Mulberry A

Post storm photograph of Mulberry A. Wrecked by the storm of June 19th-21st, elements of the wrecked Mulberry were rapidly salvaged and used in the completion of the British Mulberry. Here debris litters the beach.

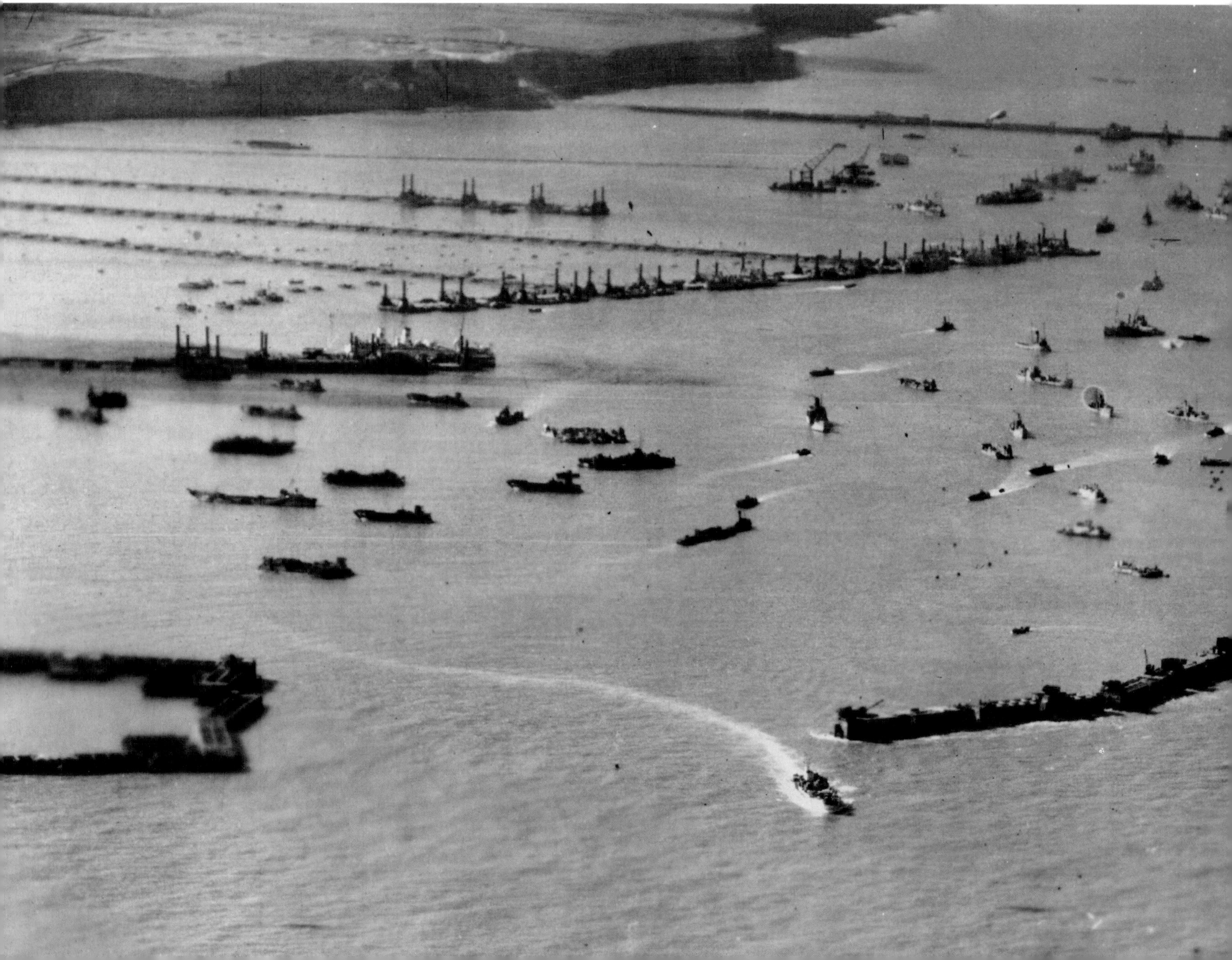

Mulberry B

A low-level oblique photograph showing the British Mulberry in operation off the town of Arromanches, at the western edge of Gold beach. Although the exact date of this photograph is not known it is sometime before the great storm that battered this area on June 19th-21st and damaged much of the port system.

Beyond the Beaches

By the end of June 6th 1944, the D-Day landings could be fairly described as an overwhelming success. Even if the Allied forces had failed to achieve some of their more ambitious objectives, the fact remains that at every beach the Atlantic Wall had been decisively breached – in some cases within as little as an hour of the first waves coming ashore. The beachheads had been established and the task now was to bring in as many reinforcements as possible ahead of the inevitable German counter-attack.

Viewed as a whole, the Allied forces had achieved this success for remarkably little loss – certainly lower than feared. There were an estimated 10,000 Allied casualties (killed, wounded, missing or captured) on D-Day in an operation that put an estimated 170,000 men into Occupied Europe on this first day alone. Of course, within this figure there were terrible losses in individual battles. US forces suffered over 2,000 casualties at Omaha on June 6th, the majority in the first waves where whole Companies were decimated before they could even get off the beach. In some sectors of Omaha, as few as 30% of the attackers even made it ashore. At Juno, similar percentage losses occurred in the first waves of Canadian forces. Casualties amongst the demolition teams, whose task it was to clear the beach barricades, were as high as 50%. Losses amongst the opposing German forces were probably lower – an estimated 7,000 men – but these came from a smaller force.

In the days following D-Day, the emphasis was on building up and consolidating the beachhead, and progress towards this goal varied enormously. Allied forces from Gold and Omaha linked within a few days to close the gap between them, but it would be nearly a week before the American divisions at Utah and Omaha connected. By now, the beachhead extended to around 15 miles inland, but would make no further advance for another six weeks.

Wounded troops being evacuated, June 8th 1944.

Army glider pilots, their work done, are evacuated from the beaches in an LCVP, June 8th 1944.

As the Allied build-up continued, the German army began to organize and counter-attack, finally pitting their tank divisions against the Allied forces. The Allies were to learn that the hedgerows of Normandy – often impenetrable barriers up to 12 feet high – were very different to the much smaller English-style hedgerows that they had been expecting. These formidable obstacles gave the occupying German forces a significant advantage, but nevertheless every counter-attack was repulsed. The overall effect of the unexpected terrain, slower-than planned advances on D-Day and the organization of German resistance was not to defeat the Allied advance but to delay it. Caen – the objective of the British forces on D-Day – was not to be taken until late July. By then German losses had risen as high as 250,000 men.

German Tiger 1 tank. The Tigers were rushed into action in August 1942 and served on all fronts until the end of the war. Annual production reached its peak of 104 in April 1944 and finally ceased in August, after 1,355 had been produced.

The German Tiger tank was one of the largest tanks of the Second World War. It weighed 56 tons and was equipped with 100mm frontal and 80mm side armor. Its main weapon, a variant of the hugely successful 88mm gun, could knock out a Sherman tank at 4,000 yards. The Tiger had been deployed with great effect on the Russian Front throughout 1943 but fortunately for the Allies on D-Day, the Tiger and the other Panzers played almost no role in defending the landing beaches. In the disputed German command system, Hitler alone had the authority to order the Panzers into action and during June 6th he failed to give the order. During the weeks that followed D-Day in the Battle for Normandy, the Tiger played a significant role in holding up the Allied breakout and knocking out Sherman tanks.

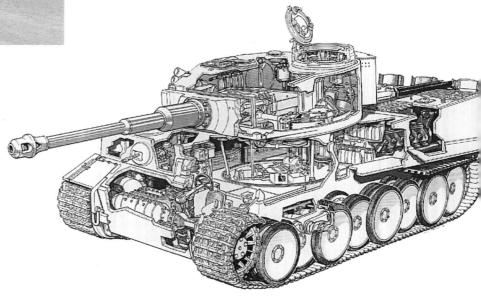

The German 88mm gun was a dual purpose weapon that could be used as an anti-tank or anti-aircraft gun. Its high muzzle velocity and long range made it one of the most deadly of German weapons. During the months before D-Day the Germans had reinforced the fortifications all along Northern France and the 88mm was integral to this. The 'Atlantic Wall' network of concrete bunkers and gun positions covered every possible landing beach from at least two angles providing enfilading fire upon the luckless first waves of landing troops. Nowhere was this defensive strategy more effective than on Omaha beach.

German Panzer IV Medium Tank. First produced in 1934, over 9,000 Panzer IV tanks were built using the same basic chassis. The Panzer IV had a good power-to-weight ratio, good mobility and proved to be a versatile workhorse – the chassis was used for various self-propelled guns, recovery vehicles, bridge layers and tank destroyers.

German Panther V tank. Considered to be one of the best tanks of the Second World War, the Panther V was designed to fight the Soviet T-34 which performed so well against the German Army on the Eastern Front. The Panther V combined a powerful gun, good protection and good mobility and was the match of the Allied tanks in Normandy. Over 4,500 Panther Vs were built between September 1942 and early 1945.

C-47s taking on wounded at an Allied airstrip in Normandy; August 2nd 1944.

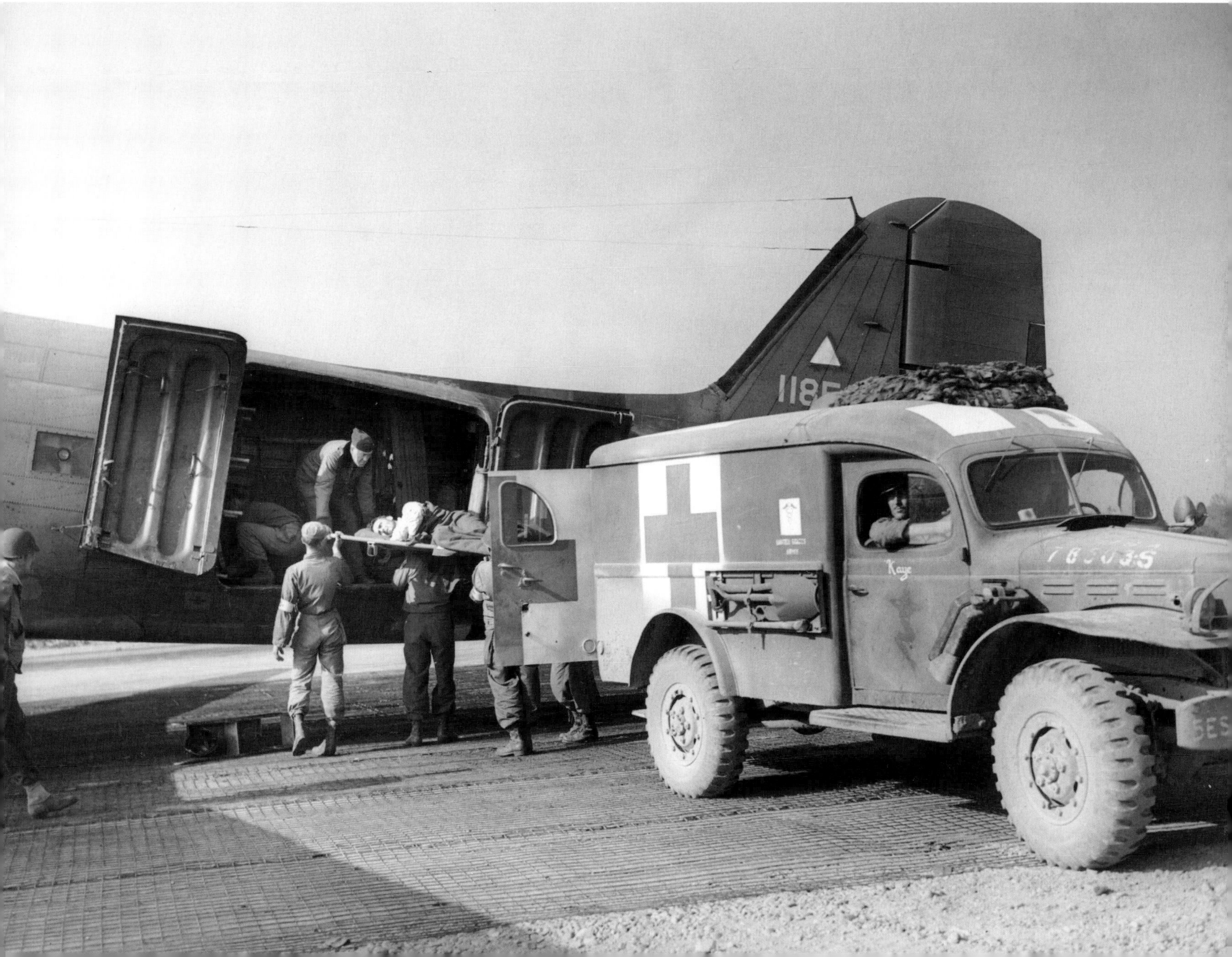

Airstrip under construction in Normandy.

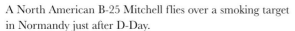
A North American B-25 Mitchell flies over a smoking target
in Normandy just after D-Day.

P-47 Thunderbolt pilots relax while an aircraft of US
412 Fighter Squadron is serviced at the Thunderbolt
Maintenance Unit in Normandy, August 1944.

From here, Allied victory in Europe was still almost a year away, with many bloody battles still to be fought. The outcome of the Second World War was not decided on June 6th 1944, but D-Day made the end of the war so much closer and so much more achievable than had seemed possible even a few months before.

D-Day did not finish the war in Europe, but it was the beginning of the end.

These men came here to storm these beaches for one purpose only. Not to gain anything for ourselves, not to fulfil any ambitions for conquest, but just to preserve freedom.

I devoutly hope that we will never again have to see such scenes as these. I prey that humanity will learn more than we had up until that time. These men bought time for us so we could do better than we had before. Every time I have come back to these beaches I say once more, we must find some way to gain eternal peace for this world.

General Eisenhower, Omaha beach, 1964

Acknowledgements

The authors record with pleasure the help of the following people and organizations in the creation of this work: Flashback Television, and in particular, Taylor Downing and David Edgar. The staff at The GeoInformation Group, in particular Julie Davenport and Paul van der Bulk who helped in the creation of the image mosaics. Seppe Cassettari is thanked for putting up with the disruptions demanded by the very short production time.

Other archive holders and organizations helped with tracking down historic materials and various images. We thank them all but especially Michael Mockford of the Medmenham Club and David Parry of the Imperial War Museum. Alan Foster and the staff of The Aerial Archives, Allan Williams and Ian McLeod are also thanked for their assistance in the creation, to tight deadlines, of imagery. In Washington DC at the US National Archives Gerry Luchansky was most helpful, as were others in his third floor team. Jeremy Pratt at Crécy is thanked for his faith and hard work in the realization of this project, while Gill Richardson has proved a tower of strength throughout. Hannah Wood is warmly thanked for providing much needed assistance with equipment at short notice also special thanks to Chris Hughes, Steve Lloyd and Dan Martin.

We must not forget the following organisations for supplying images; Art-tech, Merlin Publications, the Museum of Army Flying, RAF Museum Hendon, the Taylor Library and ww2-images.com. Chris Goss and Grub Street are also thanked for allowing us to use extracts from their books.

We thank our wives and families for their patient acceptance that the 2003 holiday season should have been filled with words and pictures relating to Operation Overlord, which took place sixty years ago this summer.

Abbreviations

ACIU	Allied Central Interpretation Unit		Lt	Lieutenant
APIS	Army Photographic Intelligence Section		mm	Millimeter/ Millimetre
AVRE	Assault Vehicle Royal Engineers		OP	Observation Point
CO	Commanding Officer		PG	Photo Group
Col	Colonel		PR	Photo Reconnaissance
CoS	Chiefs of Staff		RAF	Royal Air Force
CSM	Company Sergeant Major		RAMC	Royal Army Medical Corps
DD	Duplex Drive		RCT	Regimental Combat Team
Dr	Doctor		SBG	Small Box Girder
ECM	Electronic Counter Measures		TAF	Tactical Air Force
HMS	His Majesties Ship		US	United States
LCA	Landing Craft Assault		USAF	United States Air Force (Prior to 1947 the USAF was known as the USAAF United States Army Air Force)
LCI	Landing Craft Infantry			
LCI(L)	Landing Craft Infantry Large		USS	United States Ship
LCT	Lane Clearance Team		VC	Victoria Cross
LCVP	Landing Craft Vehicle Personnel (the 'Higgins' boat)		WN	Wiederstandnest (German strong point)
LST	Landing Ship Tank			

Further Reading

There is a vast literature on D-Day including numerous regimental works and official histories. Those wishing to learn more can also turn to a few more accessible works of reference of which the following are highly recommended:

The D-Day Encyclopaedia. David G Chandler and James Lawton Collins Jnr (Eds). Prentice Hall 1994. ISBN 0 132036 21 5

D-Day June 6th 1944. The Normandy Landings. Richard Collier. Cassell 1992 ISBN 0 297843 46 X

D-Day Then and Now Volumes 1-2. W G Ramsay (Ed). After the Battle Publications ISBN 0 900913 84 3

D-Day June 6th 1944 the climactic battle of WW2. Stephen E. Ambrose. Pocket Books 2002. ISBN 0 743449 74 6

Band of Brothers. Stephen E. Ambrose 1992. ISBN 0 671769 22 7

Allied Photo Reconnaissance of World War Two. Chris Staerck (Ed). Parkgate Books. ISBN 1 855850 01 X

Index